**the lebanese cookbook** *hussien dekmak*

# the lebanese cookbook

## hussien dekmak

photography by martin brigdale

kyle books

*I dedicate this book to the memory of my head chef at Al Hamra, Hassan Mardini, who worked very hard to make me start this journey of cooking special Lebanese food.*

This revised edition published in 2015 by Kyle Books
www.kylebooks.com
general.enquiries@kylebooks.com

Distributed by National Book Network
4501 Forbes Blvd., Suite 200
Lanham, MD 20706
Phone: (800) 462-6420
Fax: (800) 338-4550
customercare@nbnbooks.com

First published in Great Britain in 2006

10 9 8 7 6 5 4 3 2 1

ISBN 978-1-909487-23-9

Project editors: Jennifer Wheatley and Tara O'Sullivan
Designer: Geoff Hayes
Photographer: Martin Brigdale
Food styling: Hussien Dekmak (apart from pages 2, 63 and 75;
            Lucy McElvey)
Styling: Helen Trent
Copy editor: Vanessa Kendell
Editorial assistant: Vicki Murrell
Production: Nic Jones and Gemma John

Library of Congress Control Number: 2014953098

Color reproduction by Scanhouse
Printed and bound in China by C&C Offset Printing Co., Ltd.

# contents

*Introduction* 6

Soups 8

Salads 18

Cold Appetizers 32

Hot Appetizers 56

Entrées 78

Barbecues 126

Doughs, Rice, Sauces and Pickles 134

Desserts and Drinks 144

*Conversion table* 156

*Index* 157

*Acknowledgments* 160

**Welcome to Lebanon**

A beautiful country stretching across a small section of the Mediterranean sea, Lebanon is famous for its natural landscape, which combines bewitching beaches, glorious mountains and emerald green fields. *Ahlan-wasahlan* – welcome!

The temperate climate and wonderfully hospitable nature of Lebanon have produced a multitude of delicious recipes that are a pleasure to the eye and a comfort to the heart, so much so that you will want to sample each dish, especially the famous Lebanese mezze, which is known for its unique flavors. Healthy, too, with emphasis on fresh ingredients and aromatic spices, Lebanese food reflects the Mediterranean diet, with an abundance of fresh vegetables, olive oil, garlic, fish, lamb, chicken and grains.

Connoisseurs of Lebanese cuisine will tell you that is that it has exceptional qualities of both taste and variety. Tabbouleh (parsley salad); manakeish bil zahtar (flatbread baked with thyme, sumac and sesame seeds); moutabal (smoky eggplant dip); shish taouk (broiled chicken) – we've put all these and more in this book, so now you can prepare delicious, authentic meals in your own home.

**How to put a Lebanese meal together**

In Lebanon the table is always full. Soups, salads, mezze and entrées are all served at the same time and shared around, and there is always bread on the table.

The recipes in this book are traditional, home-style cooking. Most are very straightforward and you'll find you don't need many unusual ingredients. The serving sizes of dishes take into account the fact that they will be presented alongside many others, so most of the appetizers, or mezze, serve four as part of a larger meal. All Lebanese food is simple and not too heavy, and it's important that the ingredients are as fresh as possible to get the best results (every dish is prepared fresh to order in my restaurant).

You can entertain for all tastes and appetites by serving a selection of dishes from the various chapters. Although the entrées are all based around meat and fish, the other chapters provide a myriad of options for vegetarians and meat eaters alike, with wonderful salads, vegetable and lentil dishes, breads, dips and pastries.

شوربة العدس

## shorbet adas
## lentil soup

**Lentils are a real staple in Lebanon. This is a traditional Middle Eastern soup, a comforting dish to be enjoyed in the winter. Served with bread, it makes a simple family meal – my mother used to cook this for me when I was a child, and it is now my daughter's favorite. I love the way that the simple ingredients give such a depth of flavor.**

Serves 6

1 cup split red lentils, rinsed
4 tablespoons butter
1 medium onion, chopped
salt
1 tablespoon ground cumin, plus extra for garnish
lemon wedges, to serve
toasted bread, to serve

Place the lentils in a pan, cover with water and bring to a boil. Reduce the heat and cook, covered, topping up with water if necessary, for about 30 minutes.

Heat the butter in a skillet, add the onion and stir until golden. Add the onion to the lentils along with salt and the cumin. Cook a further 10 minutes, stirring.

Transfer the lentil mixture to a food processor and whizz for a few minutes until smooth.

Divide the soup among six serving bowls and sprinkle with ground cumin if desired. Serve with lemon wedges and toasted bread.

adas bil hamed
lentil soup with swiss
chard and lemon

شوربة سلق و عدس

This has been my favorite soup ever since I was a young boy. My mother used to cook it for me in the small village where I grew up. Serve this with plenty of bread and a squeeze of lemon.

Serves 4

1¹/₄ lbs Swiss chard, roughly chopped
¹/₂ cup green or brown lentils, rinsed
1 potato, cut into small cubes
salt and black pepper
1 tablespoon olive oil
2 tablespoons chopped onions
lemon juice

Place the Swiss chard in a saucepan. Add the lentils and enough water to cover, then bring to a boil and simmer, 15 minutes. Add the potato, salt and pepper and continue to cook until the lentils are cooked. Heat the olive oil in a skillet and fry the chopped onions until softened.

Add the onions to the lentils and Swiss chard, then pour in lemon juice to taste. Toss together and serve.

شوربة الخضرة

If you want to add meat, fry small pieces of lamb (about ¹/₄lb in total) with the onion at the beginning.

Serves 4

2 tablespoons butter
¹/₂ onion, diced
2 zucchinis, cut into cubes
2 carrots, cut into cubes
1 potato, cut into cubes
1 red bell pepper, seeded and diced
1 green bell pepper, seeded and diced
salt and black pepper
1 teaspoon tomato paste

Melt the butter in a saucepan, add the onion and stir until softened. Add all the other vegetables and stir until tender. Pour in enough water to cover, and season with salt and black pepper. Bring to a boil, then reduce the heat and add the tomato paste.

Stir and simmer over medium heat, a further 30 minutes. Serve hot.

# shorbet dajaj bil sha'rieh
## chicken soup with vermicelli/angel hair pasta

**In Lebanon, we only ever eat soup during the winter months. This is a hearty winter dish. Its real beauty lies in its simplicity – by using just basic ingredients, it allows the rich flavor of the chicken to come through.**

Serves 4

1/2 lb bone-in chicken breast
1 teaspoon butter
1/4 onion, chopped
salt and black pepper
2oz vermicelli or angel hair pasta
1 tablespoon chopped flat-leaf parsley

Place the chicken in a large saucepan and cover with 6 cups cold water. Bring to a boil then reduce to a simmer for about 45 minutes or until the chicken is cooked. Skim the fat from the surface, remove the chicken from the pan, and reserve the chicken stock.

Tear the chicken into pieces with your hands.

Heat the butter in a saucepan, add the onion and fry until tender. Add the reserved chicken stock with a little salt and pepper and bring to a boil. Simmer 10 minutes, then reduce the heat and add the chicken and vermicelli or angel hair pasta. Cook until the pasta is soft, a further 10–15 minutes.

Pour the soup into bowls and garnish with parsley.

When I was a young boy my family lived in a village called Bayesour in the mountains of Lebanon. My mother used to take me with her to the valley to collect special tea herbs called *zoofa* and *zaizafoon*. She mixed those with other herbs like the ones you see in the picture – dried rose petals, corn husks and bay leaves. These herbal teas or *zhoorat* are mostly drunk in the winter, to protect people from catching colds and to keep them warm. They are also sometimes drunk instead of normal tea.

شوربة الخضار بالشعير

## shorbet al khoudar bil sha'rieh
### vegetable soup with vermicelli/angel hair pasta

This comforting winter soup is a great vegetarian option. It's a simple recipe, and you can add different vegetables depending on what you like and what is available.

Serves 6

2 tablespoons vegetable oil
2 tablespoons chopped onion
1 garlic clove, crushed
3$^1$/$_2$oz dried vermicelli or angel hair pasta
1 carrot, peeled and cubed
1 zucchini, cubed
1 stick celery, chopped
1$^1$/$_2$ quarts vegetable stock
1 potato, peeled and cubed
3$^1$/$_2$oz broccoli florets
salt, to taste

Place the oil in a large saucepan and heat over high heat. Add the onion, followed by the garlic, and stir well. Reduce the heat.

Add the vermicelli or angel hair pasta and stir. Let it cook for 5 minutes, then add the carrot, zucchini and celery.

After 10 minutes, increase the heat, add the stock and bring to a boil. Add the potato and the broccoli. Bring back to a boil and simmer for about 15 minutes – enough to cook the vegetables, but making sure they retain their shape and texture. Season with salt, to taste.

Turn off the heat. Your soup is ready to be served.

This basic salad is very common in Lebanon and is great served with grilled meat dishes (see barbecue recipes on pages 126–133). Lebanese arugula is quite different to the one you find in supermarkets in the US – the leaves are much bigger and it has a sharper taste. It can be found in some specialist Middle Eastern shops, but if you can't find it, ordinary arugula also works well in this salad.

Serves 4

2 large handfuls of arugula, roughly chopped
2 tablespoons finely chopped onion
1/4 lb radishes, thinly sliced
1 large tomato, finely chopped
1 tablespoon olive oil
juice of 1/2 lemon
salt

Place the arugula in a bowl and add the onion, radishes and tomato. Add the olive oil, lemon juice and salt and mix well before serving.

Lima beans are grown all over Lebanon. They're best fresh, but people harvest and dry them so they can eat them year round. Like *foul medames* on page 58, this can be eaten as a very filling breakfast.

Serves 4

1 lb dried lima beans (lighter colored ones are best)
1/2 tablespoon fresh cilantro, finely chopped
1 teaspoon fresh Italian parsley, finely chopped
1 fresh tomato, finely chopped
3 tablespoons *tartour* (tahini sauce) (see recipe on page 140)
1 clove garlic, crushed
1 teaspoon pine nuts, toasted, to serve

Soak the beans in cold water for 7 hours, then drain and boil in fresh water for 20 minutes until fully cooked.

Drain and cool under running water. Mix the beans with the other ingredients and serve cold, topped with the pine nuts.

## salatit batata
## potato salad

**On hot days this salad makes a light lunch by itself and will serve two instead of four people.**

Serves 4

2 large potatoes, boiled
2 scallions, chopped
1 medium tomato, chopped
1 green bell pepper, seeded and chopped
1 red bell pepper, seeded and chopped
1 tablespoon chopped Italian parsley
1 teaspoon chopped mint
$^1/_2$ tablespoon lemon juice
1 tablespoon olive oil
salt

Cut the potatoes into large cubes and place in a bowl. Add the remainder of the vegetables, the herbs, lemon juice, olive oil and salt. Mix well.

Serve as an appetizer.

Lebanon is famous the world over for its olives (see below). This fresh, flavorful salad is great as an appetizer, but in Lebanon we would also serve it for breakfast, along with a plate of cheese.

Serves 4

1/3 cup kalamata or other black olives, pitted and sliced lengthwise
1/3 cup green olives, pitted and sliced lengthwise
2 tablespoons chopped scallions
1 medium tomato, chopped
1 tablespoon chopped mint
1 red bell pepper, seeded and chopped
1 tablespoon olive oil
1/2 tablespoon lemon juice
salt

Place all the ingredients in a bowl and toss together well. Serve as an appetizer.

## olive trees

Lebanon is one of the Mediterranean countries famous for growing olive trees. My brother and I used to pick olives from the trees, smash them and eat them with a little bit of salt – they are very tasty but bitter, which not everyone likes! Another way to eat them is to dip in *labneh* (see recipe on page 34) and eat as a snack.

Olive trees produce olives every two years. People who live in the mountains and have olive trees on their land harvest them and eat what they can. With the rest, half are stored in jars of oil and half are taken to the olive press in the village (*maasart zaytoon*) to make olive oil to last them until the next harvest.

# salatah al khodar al meshweya
## broiled vegetable salad

These vegetables can easily be done on a barbecue at the same time as cooking any of the other dishes in the barbecue chapter (see pages 126–133). If you are doing them this way, you will need to thread the vegetable pieces onto skewers.

Serves 4

2 tomatoes, halved
1 eggplant, cut into large pieces
1 red bell pepper, seeded and cut into large pieces
1 green bell pepper, seeded and cut into large pieces
1 onion, cut into large pieces
1 tablespoon chopped Italian parsley
1 tablespoon chopped mint leaves
1 tablespoon olive oil
1 tablespoon lemon juice
salt

Sear the vegetables under a broiler or on a barbecue until softened and charred.

Put all the broiled vegetables into a bowl. Add the parsley, mint, olive oil and lemon juice. Add salt to taste and mix together, being careful not to crush the vegetables.

Serve with barbecued meat.

## salatet al banadorah wa al basal
### tomato and onion salad

**This simple yet delicious salad makes the perfect accompaniment to the** *moujadara* **(lentils and rice with crispy onions) on page 62.**

Serves 2

3 tomatoes, roughly chopped
2 tablespoons chopped onions or scallions
salt
1 teaspoon olive oil
1 tablespoon lemon juice

Place the tomatoes, onions, salt, olive oil and lemon juice in a bowl.

Toss well together and serve.

## salatah khiar bi laban
### yogurt with cucumber dip

**The clean, fresh flavors of this simple dip make it ideal to partner with barbecued meat.**

Serves 4

3 medium cucumbers
1 cup yogurt (see recipe on page 34) or use store-bought plain yogurt
1 teaspoon dried mint
2 garlic cloves, crushed
salt

Grate the cucumbers into a bowl. Add the yogurt, mint, garlic and salt and stir to combine.

Serve with *shish taouk* (broiled chicken), *kofta meshwi* (broiled minced lamb on skewers) or with *kibbeh bil sainieh* (baked kibbeh) (see recipes on pages 129, 130 and 82).

## salatit malfouf abiad
### white cabbage salad

Lemon juice is a key ingredient in almost every Lebanese dish, in the same way that soy sauce is integral to Chinese cuisine. Here, it is used with the other classic Middle Eastern ingredients, garlic and olive oil, to make a simple dressing for crisp white cabbage.

Serves 4

1 small white cabbage
1 tablespoon olive oil
2 tablespoons lemon juice
salt
1 garlic clove, crushed

Chop the cabbage into fine strips, then place in a bowl with the olive oil, lemon juice, salt to taste and garlic. Mix well and serve.

## salatit zahtar akhdar
### fresh thyme salad

When I was a boy, my mother used to send me and my brother out into the valley near our village to gather wild thyme. Lebanese wild thyme is very different to the thyme you might find in the US – the leaves are much bigger, the size of mint leaves. If you can find it, I urge you to try it, but if not, ordinary thyme will still work beautifully in this salad.

Serves 4

$1/2$ lb fresh wild thyme (or use ordinary thyme)
2 tablespoons finely chopped onion
2 tablespoons finely chopped tomatoes
1 tablespoon lemon juice
1 teaspoon olive oil
salt

Remove the thyme leaves (you'll need around 3 cups) from the stalks and place in a dish. Add the onion, tomatoes, lemon juice, olive oil and salt to taste. Toss together well.

Serve with broiled meat dishes.

**Romaine lettuce is the most popular lettuce in Lebanon, and it's used in many of our salads. Lebanese salads are always made with large chunks, whereas countries like Syria and Armenia tend to slice their salad ingredients much more finely. This chunky salad is great with barbecued meat.**

Serves 4

1 head romaine lettuce
1 cucumber
1 medium tomato
small handful of finely chopped mint
2 tablespoons finely chopped Italian parsley
1 tablespoon lemon juice
2 teaspoons olive oil
salt

Cut the lettuce, cucumber and tomato into large chunks and place in a large bowl.

Add the mint and parsley, then pour in the lemon juice and olive oil. Season with salt and toss together well. Serve immediately.

**Lebanese salads rarely use chile, so this spicy salad is more Arabic in style.**

Serves 4

2 small cucumbers
1 head romaine lettuce, roughly chopped
2 tomatoes, roughly chopped
1 teaspoon finely chopped hot green chili pepper
1 teaspoon olive oil
1 tablespoon lemon juice
1 garlic clove, crushed
salt

Cut the cucumbers into quarters lengthwise, then chop them widthwise.

Place the cucumber pieces in a bowl along with the lettuce, tomatoes and chili pepper. Add the olive oil, lemon juice, garlic and salt to taste and mix together.

Serve with broiled meat or fish.

Making your own yogurt is easy and it's much cheaper than buying it ready-made. It will keep in the fridge for about a week and is used for some other dishes in this book; *salatah khiar bi laban* (yogurt with cucumber dip) (see recipe on page 28) and *laban ayran* (yogurt drink) (see recipe on page 154). *Laban* is also served alongside other mezze.

    *Labneh* can be made by putting *laban* in cheesecloth or muslin and leaving it to drain overnight. This makes a thicker yogurt and is served with *manakeish bil zahtar* and *manakeish bil jibneh* for breakfast (see recipes on pages 69–70).

Makes 4$^{1}/_{2}$ lbs

8 cups whole milk
2 tablespoons plain yogurt

Pour the milk into a saucepan and bring to a boil. Simmer over medium heat for 10 minutes, then set aside to cool, about 30 minutes.

Add the yogurt to the milk and stir well. Cover the pan with a lid and then wrap it up well in a blanket. Set aside in a warm place for 6 hours.

Remove the lid and place the pan in the refrigerator for 2 hours before serving.

This recipe makes a large batch of hummus that will keep for one week in the fridge. The baking soda of soda helps the chickpeas to cook quickly and also helps loosen their skins so they can be easily removed. Just make sure you rinse the chickpeas well after cooking to get rid of any traces of the baking soda. Once refrigerated, the hummus thickens, so make it quite thin to start with. The ice is used to keep the food processor cool.

Buy good-quality tahini. Good tahini shouldn't taste too bitter. The cheaper brands use peanuts and don't taste good.

Serves 4

2²/3 cups dried chickpeas, soaked overnight and rinsed
2 tablespoons baking soda
salt
1/4 lb ice
1 cup tahini
1/4 cup lemon juice

Place the chickpeas in a large saucepan with plenty of fresh cold water and the baking soda. Bring to a boil and simmer for about 45 minutes until soft to the touch. Remove the pan from the heat and stir well to loosen the skins from the beans. Drain away the water and skins so you are just left with the beans. Rinse thoroughly.

Place the beans in a food processor and whizz with a little salt to a smooth paste.

Add the ice, tahini and some of the lemon juice. Whizz again, adding about 2 cups of water in a steady stream, until the mixture is smooth and the consistency of a creamy paste. Pour in the remaining lemon juice and add more salt to taste.

## smoky eggplant dip

### moutabal

متبل باذنجان

Also known as *baba ghanoush* in Syria and Egypt. Charring the eggplants on a gas flame or charcoal grill gives the dip a distinctive smoky flavor. Be careful not to overdo the tahini; you only need a little to bring out the flavor of the eggplants.

Serves 4

2 large eggplants
1/4 cup tahini
1 tablespoon lemon juice
salt
olive oil, to drizzle
1 tablespoon pomegranate seeds (optional)

Char the eggplants directly over a gas flame or over charcoal, using tongs, until the flesh is tender. Peel under cold running water and discard the skins. Allow the eggplants to cool to room temperature.

Finely chop the eggplants and place in a bowl. Add the tahini, lemon juice and salt to taste, and mix well.

Drizzle a little olive oil on top and sprinkle with pomegranate seeds, if using.

**The chile in this dish gives it an essential kick – I really think the spiciness works well here. All those nuts also mean that *muhamara* is great for energy.**

Serves 6

vegetable oil, for deep-frying
1/2 cup pistachio nuts
1 cup walnuts
1/2 cup cashew nuts
1/2 cup blanched almonds
1/2 cup pine nuts (optional)
2 tablespoons finely chopped onion
1 red bell pepper, seeded and finely chopped
1 tablespoon finely chopped Italian parsley
4 cups fresh bread crumbs
1 green chili pepper, finely chopped (or 2 teaspoons chilli powder)
1 cup olive oil
salt and black pepper

Heat the oil in a deep-fat fryer or deep, heavy-bottomed saucepan. Deep-fry the nuts for a matter of minutes – any longer and the walnuts will taste bitter. Drain and set aside to cool.

Finely chop the nuts and place in a bowl with the onion, red pepper, parsley, bread crumbs, chili pepper and olive oil. Season with salt and pepper and mix well. Serve.

*Along with* tabbouleh *(page 48),* fattoush *has to be one of the main salads in Lebanese culture. Its distinctive flavor comes from sumac. Berries are gathered from the large sumac trees, then dried and ground into this spice. This salad is substantial enough to be eaten by itself as a light lunch.*

Serves 4

1 carrot, chopped
1/2 head romaine lettuce, chopped
1 cucumber, chopped
2 tomatoes, chopped
5 radishes, chopped
1 tablespoon chopped scallion
1 red bell pepper, seeded and chopped
1 garlic clove, minced
1 tablespoon chopped Italian parsley
2 teaspoons sumac
1 large flatbread, toasted and broken into pieces
2–3 tablespoons olive oil
salt

Combine all the vegetables in a large bowl and mix well. Add the garlic, parsley, sumac, bread, olive oil and salt to taste. Toss everything together and serve immediately.

foul moukala
fava beans with garlic
and cilantro فول مقلى

I use frozen fava beans for this recipe; they give a better texture than fresh. Wait until the beans are cooled before mixing with the garlic – you'll preserve the garlic's splendor this way.

Serves 4

1¼ lbs shelled fava beans
1 teaspoon minced garlic
2 tablespoons chopped cilantro
2 tablespoons olive oil
salt and black pepper

Bring the beans to a boil, then simmer until tender, 30 minutes. Drain and set aside to cool.

Place the beans in a bowl with the garlic, cilantro, olive oil, salt and pepper. Mix well and serve.

fouter moukala
fried mushrooms with
garlic and cilantro فطر مقلى

Serves 4

vegetable oil, for deep-frying
1¼ lbs mushrooms, thinly sliced
1 tablespoon olive oil
1 teaspoon minced garlic
2 tablespoons chopped cilantro
salt and black pepper
½ teaspoon ground coriander

Heat the vegetable oil in a deep-fat fryer or deep, heavy-bottomed saucepan. Add the mushrooms and fry for about 10 minutes, stirring occasionally, until golden brown and crisp. Remove with a slotted spoon and set aside.

Heat the olive oil in a pan over low heat. Add the garlic and cilantro and cook, stirring, 10 minutes. Add the fried mushrooms, salt, pepper and ground coriander and stir together. Serve hot or cold.

## batinjan makdous
## pickled eggplants

My wife's mother makes the best *batinjan makdous*. She does big batches of 20 lbs of eggplant at a time to keep for the year and we always bring home a few jars after we've visited. As they keep for a long time (at least two months), it's worth making a big batch. You will need a few large jars with airtight lids. See picture on page 40.

about 2 lbs small eggplants (about 15–20), stalks removed
2 cups walnuts, finely chopped
1 teaspoon finely chopped green chili pepper
2 small green bell peppers, seeded and finely chopped
2 small red bell peppers, seeded and finely chopped
4 garlic cloves, finely chopped
salt
plenty of olive oil

Place the eggplants in a large pan, cover with water and bring to a boil. Cook until soft but still holding their shape, approximately 20 minutes. Drain and drop immediately into a pan of cold water to cool. Drain and set aside.

In a bowl, mix together the walnuts, chili pepper, bell peppers, garlic and a pinch of salt.

Make a slit lengthwise (not quite end to end) in each eggplant, cutting halfway down the vegetable. Place a little stuffing inside the eggplant. Repeat until all the eggplants are stuffed, then tightly pack the eggplants into glass jars, filling right to the top.

Turn each jar over a strainer or colander to drain any excess liquid and leave overnight.

Pour enough olive oil into each jar to cover the eggplants. They will be ready to serve after 3 weeks.

**Lebanese seven spice, or *sabaa baharat,* is a combination of cloves, cumin, nutmeg, ground coriander, cinnamon and pepper with paprika often added for color. It can be bought in Mediterranean or Middle Eastern stores.**

1 cup Arborio rice
3 medium tomatoes, chopped
2 onions, chopped
half a bunch of Italian parsley, chopped
1 tablespoon chopped mint
3 tablespoons lemon juice
generous $1/2$ cup olive oil
salt
$1/2$ teaspoon Lebanese seven spice mix
10 small eggplants, stalks removed
4 medium potatoes, sliced into $3/4$ inch-thick rounds

Place the rice in a bowl with the tomatoes, onions, parsley and mint. Add the lemon juice, 3 tablespoons of the olive oil, plus the salt and spice mix and mix well.

Hollow out the eggplants, then stuff the eggplants with the rice mixture.

Place the potato slices in the bottom of a saucepan large enough to hold the potato slices in one layer. Lay the stuffed eggplants on top in one layer and pour in the remaining olive oil and enough water to cover the eggplants by $3/4$ inch. Take a heavy heatproof plate just large enough to fit inside the pan and press down – this stops the eggplants from floating around. Place extra weight on the plate if needed.

Bring to a boil, then reduce the heat and cook, about $1^1/2$ hours.

Remove the eggplants and leave to cool (use the potatoes for another dish). Serve cold.

# market

Oranges, lemons and bananas are some of Lebanon's exports. My father goes every day to these markets to buy fruits and vegetables. These days when you place an order you can find grocers who will prepare your vegetables – chop parsley, hollow out zucchini, peel carrots and take the Jew's mallow leaves off the stem and put them in a bag for you. You can go back in an hour and everything is ready. Of course, they charge more but it saves a lot of time.

Above: a traditional store with a hairdresser's on the right. You can find these shops in every quarter in Beirut because we don't have many big supermarkets. You can also see the word *safa* on the walls – this is a soccer team in the mountains.

Right: spices for sale – from top left going clockwise: *falafel* spices, turmeric, *kebseh* spices, *frakeh* spices, cinnamon and paprika. The spice in the bottom left looks like *zahtar,* but is, in fact, a spice mix that is used in *frakeh,* a traditional dish from the south of Lebanon that my mother often makes, which is based around raw lamb. *Kebseh* is a dish made with chicken or lamb together with rice.

## batinjan rahib
### eggplant salad

The combination of vegetables and walnut in this salad makes for a beautiful taste and a great texture. Eggplant is famous in Lebanon and you'll notice that it features in many of the dishes in this book. Some people serve this salad hot, but I think that letting it cool before serving really brings out the smoky flavor of the charred eggplants.

Serves 4

2 medium eggplants
2 medium tomatoes, finely chopped
1 tablespoon finely chopped onion
1 tablespoon chopped Italian parsley
1 garlic clove, minced
1 tablespoon finely chopped walnuts
1 tablespoon lemon juice
$1/2$ tablespoon olive oil
salt
1 tablespoon pomegranate seeds (optional)

Char the eggplants directly over a gas flame until the flesh is tender. Peel the skins under cold running water and discard. Allow the eggplants to cool to room temperature, then finely chop them.

Put the tomatoes, onion and parsley in a bowl and combine with the eggplants, garlic, walnuts, lemon juice, olive oil and salt to taste.

Mix all the ingredients and top with pomegranate seeds, if using. Serve immediately.

# tabbouleh
## parsley salad

تبولة

Another classic Lebanese salad, I think this is second only to hummus in terms of international popularity. Use fine bulgur wheat if you can get it but, if not, regular bulgur wheat will do. Remember, parsley is the main ingredient in this salad, so make sure it is fresh and fragrant.

Serves 4

1 tablespoon fine bulgur wheat
1 tablespoon finely chopped onion
juice of 2 lemons
$1/4$ cup olive oil
4 tomatoes, finely chopped
6 cups finely chopped Italian parsley
1 tablespoon finely chopped mint leaves
salt and black pepper

Soak the bulgur wheat in a little cold water to soften, 5 minutes. Place in a bowl with the onion, lemon juice, olive oil, tomatoes, parsley and mint – the bulgur wheat will soak up the other juices in the salad.
Add salt and pepper to taste and serve.

warak einab bi zeit
stuffed grape leaves in oil
رق عنب بالزيت

Lebanon is famous for its vines. Wine has been produced here for thousands of years, and we use the vine leaves to make this classic dish, which is served cold with *laban* (see recipe on page 34). You can buy grape, or vine, leaves in brine from most supermarkets.

Serves 4

1 1/2 cups Arborio rice, rinsed
2 tablespoons finely chopped mint
2 medium onions, finely chopped
5 medium tomatoes, finely chopped
a bunch of Italian parsley, finely chopped
1/4 cup lemon juice
1/4 cup olive oil
salt and Lebanese seven spice mix (see page 43)
1 jar (1/2 lb) grape leaves, rinsed
2 medium potatoes, peeled and sliced into rounds

Mix the rice in a bowl with the mint, onions, tomatoes and parsley, then add the lemon juice, olive oil, salt and Lebanese seven spice mix. Place the mixture in a strainer over a bowl and leave to drain, 10–15 minutes. Reserve the liquid.

Lay the grape leaves out on a board. Place a tablespoon of the stuffing near the stem end of each grape leaf. Fold the bottom and sides of the leaf over the stuffing and roll up firmly to give a cigar shape. Repeat with the other grape leaves.

Place the potato rounds in the bottom of a large, heavy-bottomed saucepan and pack the stuffed grape leaves closely together on top, in layers.

Put a heavy heatproof plate that fits inside the pan on top, to keep the rolls in shape during cooking. Place a heatproof bowl filled with water on top to add extra weight. Pour in the reserved liquid and enough water to cover the plate by a 3/4 inch.

Cover with a lid and bring to a boil, then reduce the heat and cook very gently, 1 1/2 hours.

Drain the liquid from the pan. Serve the grape leaves cold with *laban* (yogurt) (see recipe on page 34) and with the cooked potatoes, too, if you wish.

## loubia bi zeit
## green beans with tomato

**Although this makes a great vegetarian dish when served cold, you could also cook it with meat and serve it hot with rice on the side to make a hearty main.**

Serves 4

3 tablespoons olive oil
1/2 onion, finely chopped
3 garlic cloves, chopped
1 1/4 lbs green beans, each cut into three pieces
5 ripe tomatoes, chopped
1 tablespoon tomato paste, mixed in 1 1/2 cups water
salt and black pepper
scallions, sliced, to serve

Heat the olive oil in a saucepan and fry the onion and garlic until softened. Add the green beans and cook, stirring occasionally, 5 minutes.

Add the tomatoes and stir occasionally until tender. Stir in the tomato paste mixture and salt and pepper to taste. Bring the mixture to a boil, then cook over low heat, 45 minutes. Serve cold with scallions.

## fasoulieh bi zeit
## beans in oil

Serves 4

scant 1 cup dried cannellini beans (white kidney beans)
1 tablespoon lemon juice
1 teaspoon minced garlic
salt
2 tablespoons olive oil

Soak the beans overnight in cold water. Drain and rinse, then place in a pan. Cover with cold water and bring to a boil. Simmer until cooked, about 30 minutes, then drain and set aside to cool.

Transfer the beans to a serving dish and toss with the remainder of the ingredients. Mix well and serve.

We also use the name *Asoura* for this dish, which means "squeezed" – because of the way you squeeze the chicory. I like to eat this with bread and olives to make a simple meal. You could completely change this dish with the simple addition of onion – instead of boiling the chicory, fry it in a pan with some onion and olive oil.

Serves 4

3/4 lb chicory (curly endive or radicchio), roughly chopped
olive oil
lemon juice
salt

Bring the chicory to a boil in a saucepan full of water. Boil until soft, 15 minutes. Drain and set aside to cool.

Squeeze out the water with your hands until the chicory is dry. Form into balls about 2 inches wide. At this stage you can put the chicory in the refrigerator – it will keep for about a week like this.

When ready to serve, place a ball on a plate, flatten out and drizzle with olive oil and lemon juice. Season with salt to taste.

## moussaka bi zeit
## eggplant and tomato moussaka

**This is one of my favorite dishes. It's a traditional and easy recipe, one that I always cook for vegetarians. The eggplants are cooked twice, giving them lots of flavor. Although I've included it as a cold appetizer, you could also serve it hot with a side of rice to turn it into a great vegetarian entrée.**

Serves 4

3–4 eggplants
vegetable oil, for deep-frying
1 cup cooked chickpeas
scant $^1/_2$ cup olive oil
6 garlic cloves, finely sliced
1 onion, finely sliced
2 (15oz) cans chopped tomatoes
2 tablespoons tomato paste
salt and black pepper
2 large tomatoes, sliced

Preheat the oven to 350°F.

Peel the eggplant lengthwise with a potato peeler, leaving long stripes of skin. Cut each one in half widthwise and then slice the two halves lengthwise.

Heat the oil in a deep-fat fryer or deep, heavy-bottomed saucepan. Deep-fry the eggplant slices until browned. Remove with a slotted spoon and spread out in a deep ovenproof tray in one layer. Spread the chickpeas on top of the eggplant slices.

Heat the olive oil separately and cook the garlic and onion until softened. Add the chopped tomatoes, the tomato paste and salt and pepper to taste. Stir and cook over low heat, 30 minutes.

Pour the tomato mixture over the chickpeas. Arrange the sliced tomatoes over the top, then bake in the oven, 30 minutes. Cut into pieces and serve cold, or hot with rice.

## barassia
## leeks in oil

The head chef at Al Hamra in Mayfair taught me how to make this dish
when I came to the UK 26 years ago. Although leeks are not a classic
Lebanese vegetable, the addition of olive oil, garlic and cilantro gives them a
Middle Eastern feel. Eat this straight away, still hot, with a squeeze of
lemon.

Serves 4

1¼ lbs leeks, cut into chunks
3 tablespoons olive oil
3 garlic cloves, minced
1 tablespoon chopped cilantro
salt and black pepper

Bring a saucepan of water to a boil and cook the leeks until tender, 15
minutes. Drain and set aside to cool.

Heat the olive oil in a pan and gently cook the garlic until softened. Add the
cilantro, salt and pepper and cook for a few more minutes, stirring. Add this
mixture to the leeks and mix well. Serve immediately.

## bamia bi zeit
## okra in oil

Use baby okra, which are ¹/₂ inch to 1 inch long and can be bought frozen.

Serves 4

vegetable oil, for deep-frying
1¼ lbs baby okra
3 tablespoons olive oil
¹/₂ onion, finely chopped
5 garlic cloves, minced
5–6 ripe tomatoes, chopped
2 tablespoons tomato paste, mixed in 1 cup water
salt and black pepper
a large handful of cilantro, chopped

Heat the oil in a deep-fat fryer or deep, heavy-bottomed saucepan. Deep-fry
the okra until browned. Set aside to cool.

Heat the olive oil in a pan, then add the onion and garlic and stir occasionally
until browned. Add the tomatoes and cook over medium heat until tender,
then add the tomato paste mixture and salt and pepper to taste. Cook for
20 minutes, then stir through the cilantro and cook over low heat for a
further 15 minutes. Stir in the okra and set aside to cool. Serve cold.

**These look similar to the stuffed grape leaves on page 49, but the flavors are so different. This recipe isn't as popular as the one for stuffed grape leaves, but you'll still see it cooked in many places in Lebanon.**

Serves 4

*for the stuffing*
1½ cups Arborio rice, rinsed
2 onions, chopped
5 medium tomatoes, chopped
2 handfuls of Italian parsley, chopped
½ cup cooked chickpeas
3 tablespoons lemon juice
3–4 tablespoons olive oil
salt and black pepper

3½ lbs Swiss chard
3 tablespoons olive oil

For the stuffing, place the rice in a bowl with the other stuffing ingredients. Mix together and transfer to a strainer placed over a bowl to catch the mixture's juices. Drain about 15 minutes.

Cut off the stalk ends of the Swiss chard and place them in a deep saucepan (this is to protect the leaves from burning during cooking). Drop the leaves into a pan of boiling water. Blanch for a minute or two, then drain and leave to cool slightly.

Lay out the Swiss chard leaves on a board. Put 1 tablespoon of the stuffing on each leaf, tuck in the ends and roll up firmly.

Place the filled leaves in the pan on the top of the stalk ends. Cover with a heavy heatproof plate that fits inside the pan (this packs the stuffed leaves down so they hold their shape). Add the reserved soaking juice and olive oil to the pan and pour in enough water to cover the plate by ¾ inch. Bring to a boil, then reduce the heat to very low and cook, 1½ hours.

Drain the stuffed leaves and discard the stalks. Serve cold with *laban* (yogurt) (see recipe on page 34).

# foul medames
## fava beans with garlic and chickpeas

**We usually eat this for breakfast with yogurt, soft cheese and olives. It is quite filling and you'll find you don't need lunch! If you are short of time, use two cans of fava beans and one can of chickpeas instead of dried.**

Serves 4

**1 cup dried fava beans**
**1/2 cup dried chickpeas**
**1 teaspoon baking soda**
**2 garlic cloves, minced**
**juice of 2 lemons**
**1 teaspoon ground cumin**
**salt**
**olive oil**
**1 tablespoon chopped Italian parsley**

Soak the fava beans and chickpeas in separate bowls for 8 hours or overnight.

Drain the fava beans, rinse and place in a saucepan. Cover with water and bring to a boil. Cook for about 45 minutes or until tender.

Meanwhile, bring a separate pan of water to a boil and add the baking soda and drained chickpeas. Cook until tender, about 40 minutes. Rinse under cold water to remove the baking soda, then boil again in fresh water a further 5 minutes. Drain.

Drain the fava beans and place in a bowl with the chickpeas. Roughly mash with a spoon or pestle, then add the garlic, lemon juice, cumin and salt to taste. Mix well.

Transfer to a serving dish and finish with olive oil and parsley. Serve with lettuce, tomatoes, scallions, radishes and pickles.

# jibneh bil za'atar
## halloumi with za'atar

**Although this makes a great starter, in Lebanon many people would eat it for breakfast. Halloumi is a popular cheese to cook with because it holds its shape rather than melting. The za'atar used here gives the cheese a fresh lemon taste which complements its saltiness.**

Serves 2–3

1 tablespoon vegetable oil
9oz block halloumi cheese, cut into 8 slices
1 teaspoon za'atar, to serve

Heat the oil in a frying pan. Once it is hot, add the slices of halloumi and shallow fry them until they become brown, turning occasionally.

Remove from the heat and place on a serving plate. Sprinkle with the za'atar and serve with slices of tomato, onion and cucumber.

The word *awarma* in this recipe title refers to the meat in this dish. In the winter, people who live in remote villages in Lebanon often find they are cut off by the snow. They prepare this meat by cooking it and preserving it in jars, so they can eat it throughout the winter. However, you can create this dish using fresh meat, just as I have here. If you want to leave the lamb out, you can turn this into *hummus snouber* – another popular dish.

Serves 4

1 quantity *hummus bil tahina* (see recipe on page 35)
1 tablespoon vegetable oil
1/4 lb lamb shoulder, cut into 1/2-inch pieces
1 teaspoon pine nuts
salt and black pepper

Place the hummus in a serving dish and use a tablespoon to make a well in the center.

Heat the vegetable oil in a skillet and fry the lamb and pine nuts, 5–7 minutes. Stir well, then add salt and pepper and cook until the meat is tender.

Arrange the meat and pine nuts in the well of the hummus and sprinkle with more black pepper.

# moujadara
## lentils and rice with crispy onions

**I love this recipe and take it with me wherever I go. For years, I cooked it at my restaurant Le Mignon in Camden, and now I cook it at my new restaurant, the Mia Lounge. The cumin gives it real impact and the textures of the lentils and rice with the crispy onions is fantastic. Lentils are such a staple food in Lebanon and I think this recipe shows them at their very best. You can use either green or brown lentils, but I find that brown lentils give a much better result.**

Serves 4

generous 1 cup brown or green dried lentils, rinsed
1/4 cup olive oil
1/2 small onion, finely chopped
1/2 cup basmati rice
salt and black pepper
1 teaspoon ground cumin

*for the crispy onions*
vegetable oil
4 tablespoons sliced onion

Place the lentils in a deep saucepan, cover with water and bring to a boil. Boil for 20 minutes, then drain and set aside.

Heat the olive oil in a lidded saucepan, add the chopped onion and fry until browned. Add the rice, cooked lentils, salt, pepper and cumin and just enough water to cover. Cover and bring to a boil, then reduce the heat and stir occasionally until the rice is cooked, 15 minutes. Place in a serving dish.

For the crispy onions, pour vegetable oil into a deep skillet to the depth of about 2 inches. Heat well and deep-fry the sliced onion until brown and crispy. Remove from the skillet and arrange on top of the lentil and rice mixture. Serve hot.

Every cuisine the world over has its own kind of pastry dish. This is the classic Lebanese one. Always make the dough yourself using my recipe on page 138 – you really won't get the same result by using ready-made pastry. Unlike the spinach and cheese pastries on the following pages, these meat pasties shouldn't be baked in the oven – they are best deep-fried. They can be stored in the freezer for up to 3 weeks.

Serves 4 plus extra for freezing

*for the stuffing*
2 tablespoons vegetable oil
3/4 lb ground lamb
1 medium onion, chopped
1 cup pine nuts
salt and black pepper
1 teaspoon ground cinnamon
2oz *labneh* (see recipe on page 34)
1 tablespoon finely chopped Italian parsley

1 batch pastry dough (see recipe on page 138)
flour, for dusting
vegetable oil, for deep-frying

Start by preparing the stuffing. Heat the oil in a large sauté pan and cook the lamb, stirring occasionally, until browned. Add the onion, pine nuts, salt, pepper and cinnamon and cook for a further 25 minutes. Spread out in a large baking tray so that the mixture cools quickly.

When the meat mixture has cooled, transfer to a bowl and add the labneh and parsley. Mix well.

Roll out the dough on a floured surface as thinly as possible. Cut into 4-inch rounds.

Put 1 1/2 teaspoons of the stuffing in the middle of each dough circle. Fold over one side to make semicircles. Seal the edges together using the tines of a fork and make a pattern around the edge. (The pastries can be frozen at this stage by placing them on a floured baking sheet.)

Heat the oil in a deep-fat fryer or deep, heavy-bottomed saucepan. Slide in the pastries and cook until golden brown, about 5–7 minutes.

Drain and serve hot or cold.

# sambousak jibneh
## cheese pastries

These pastries can be cooked straight from frozen. Simply place the pastries on a floured baking tray before freezing.

If you don't want to deep-fry, cut the pastry into rectangles, place the stuffing in the center and pinch the sides to make small boats. Then bake in a medium oven for about 15 minutes or until golden brown.

Serves 4 plus extra for freezing

*for the stuffing*
3/4 lb halloumi or feta cheese, shredded
2 tablespoons chopped flat-leaf parsley
3 tablespoons butter, melted

1 batch pastry dough (see recipe on page 138)
flour, for dusting
vegetable oil, for deep-frying

Rinse the halloumi if you find it too salty. Place the halloumi in a bowl, add the parsley and melted butter and mix well until it all sticks together.

Divide the dough into walnut-size balls. Roll out each ball on a floured surface as thinly as possible.

Put a tablespoon or so of stuffing in the middle of each dough circle. Fold in half, corner to corner, and seal well in a crescent shape.

Heat the oil in a deep-fat fryer or deep, heavy-bottomed saucepan. Gently lower the pastries into the hot oil and deep-fry until golden, about 5–10 minutes. Serve hot.

These spinach pastries are my favorite of the three pastries in this book. In Lebanon, they sell large versions of these pastries for breakfast. The street seller hands them to you wrapped in paper, and you just bite straight into your pastry on the street. These pastries are the Lebanese equivalent of fast food – although if you visit nowadays you'll see plenty of branded burger bars springing up alongside the traditional street sellers! These pastries freeze well (just place them on a baking tray wiped with a little vegetable oil or flour and place in the freezer), so it's a good idea to make a big batch, then just fry or bake them when needed.

Serves 8

*for the stuffing*
2 lbs fresh spinach
salt and black pepper
2 medium onions, finely chopped
2 tablespoons pine nuts
1/4 cup sumac
juice of 2 lemons
scant 1/2 cup olive oil

1 batch pastry dough (see recipe on page 138)
flour, for dusting
vegetable oil, for deep-frying

Wash the spinach well. Finely chop and place in a bowl. Sprinkle with salt and rub well with your hands until soft. Squeeze to drain excess water. Add the onions, pine nuts, sumac, lemon juice, olive oil, salt and pepper and mix well. Drain the excess liquid to get a thick and dry stuffing.

Roll out the dough on a floured surface as thinly as possible. Cut into rounds using a 4-inch cookie cutter.

Place a tablespoon of the spinach filling in the middle of each circle. Bring up the edges at 3 points to form a triangular shape. Press the edges firmly together with your fingertips to seal completely.

Heat the vegetable oil in a deep-fat fryer or deep, heavy-bottomed saucepan and deep-fry the pastries until golden brown, about 5 minutes. Drain, leave to cool slightly and serve warm. Alternatively, bake in a 350°F oven for about 10–15 minutes.

## manakeish bil zahtar
### bread baked with thyme

*Manakeish bil zahtar, manakeish bil jibneh* and *lahma bi ajeen* (see recipes on pages 70–71) are often eaten for breakfast in Lebanon with black tea. *Zahtar* (or za'atar) is a mixture of wild thyme, sumac and toasted sesame seeds. I buy it ready mixed from Lebanon. You can find it in Middle Eastern food stores and most supermarkets.

Serves 4

1/4 cup za'atar, with a little extra sumac added
6 tablespoons olive oil, plus extra for greasing
6–8 balls bread dough (see recipe on page 136)
2 tablespoons all-purpose flour

Preheat the oven to 350°F.

Place the za'atar and olive oil in a bowl and mix. Sprinkle the dough balls with flour, then roll out on a board into 1/4-inch thick disks. Place on an oiled baking sheet.

Spread a little of the za'atar mixture over each piece of dough. Make indents with your fingers all over the dough to stop the bread from puffing up during cooking.

Bake in the oven until the bread is golden brown, about 10 minutes. Be careful as the *zahtar* burns quite quickly.

Serve with cucumbers, tomatoes, olives and fresh mint.

## manakeish bil jibneh
### baked dough with cheese

This is another "fast food" dish. It's big and quick and, served with black tea, will definitely keep you going. In Lebanon we use a cheese called *akewi*, which comes in big, square blocks. It's very salty, so has to be soaked in water first. Then the street sellers grate it and spread it over the dough (often very finely, to try and save money!). It's difficult to find *akewi* in the West, but halloumi or feta would work just as well for this dish. See picture on page 68.

Serves 4

³/₄ lb halloumi or feta cheese
6–8 balls bread dough (see recipe on page 138)
2 tablespoons all-purpose flour
1 tablespoon melted butter, plus extra for greasing
1 teaspoon sesame seeds

Preheat the oven to 350°F.

Wash the cheese to get rid of the salt. Cut into thin slices.

Sprinkle the dough balls with flour, then roll out into 6-inch disks. Place on a greased baking sheet.

Brush the butter over the dough using a pastry brush. Divide the slices of cheese between the disks. Sprinkle with sesame seeds, then use your fingers to make indents in the dough – this stops the bread from puffing up in the oven. Bake in the oven until the bread is golden around the edges, about 10 minutes.

Serve with olives and cucumbers.

**Although some Lebanese people will eat these for breakfast, they're also good for a quick lunch, served with** *laban* **(yogurt) or** *laban ayran* **(yogurt drink, see pages 34 and 154). These little pizza-style breads are very popular in Lebanon and also in Syria, but you'll notice that the thickness of the dough varies a lot from place to place.**

Serves 4

1/4 onion
2 tomatoes
1 small green chili pepper
1/3 lb finely ground lamb
1 tablespoon tomato paste
salt and black pepper
6–8 balls bread dough (see recipe on page 136)
2 tablespoons all-purpose flour
1 teaspoon olive oil, for greasing
1 tablespoon pine nuts

Preheat the oven to 350°F.

Whiz the onion, tomatoes and green chili in a food processor to a fine paste. Transfer to a bowl and add the lamb, tomato paste, salt and pepper and mix well.

Sprinkle the dough balls with flour and roll out into disks as thinly as you can. Place the dough circles on an oiled baking sheet. Spread some of the meat mixture on each circle, then sprinkle over the pine nuts. Bake in the oven, about 15 minutes. Serve.

Left: This bread is very popular in Lebanon. It is called *ka'ak*. People like to walk along the corniche in Beirut in the evening or afternoon. They buy bread or nuts, and often an espresso as well, and sometimes sit out until late at night. You can buy *ka'ak* at any time of day – and it is much cheaper than going to a restaurant! For breakfast, they put soft cheese inside, so it melts, or you could have it with za'atar. It will fill you up for the whole day. The hole you see in the top of this bread is simply there to hold it by! This bread is one of the things I miss most about Lebanon – filling and delicious, stuffed with anything you want, from cheese to salami.

When I go to Lebanon on holiday each year I like to go to a bakery called abu Arab in Al-Naameh in the south, by the sea. There you can find the best *ka'ak* in Lebanon. They start making the dough very early in the morning and sell the *ka'ak* all day long. They are huge but I always find I can eat two!

Below: Another popular snack is nuts, and you can buy many different kinds and flavors from sellers like this one – pistachios, cashews, peanuts, watermelon seeds, pumpkin seeds, roasted chickpeas and barbecued almonds are all on offer, which you can buy with or without salt added. The pink ones in the picture are roasted chickpeas covered with sugar, which are very popular with children.

## falafel
### fava bean patties

Falafel is such a famous dish. When I first started cooking it in the UK, people didn't know what was in it. It's growing in popularity here now, but many people still don't realize how easy it is to make. In Lebanon, there are shops that sell only falafel. We eat it in wraps, with tomato, pickle and tahini sauce.

Serves 4

1 cup dried fava beans, soaked overnight, then rinsed and drained
1/2 cup dried chickpeas, soaked overnight, then rinsed and drained
1/2 onion
1/2 red bell pepper, seeded
3 tablespoons roughly chopped fresh cilantro
5 garlic cloves
1 teaspoon ground cumin
2 tablespoons ground coriander
1 teaspoon baking soda
1 teaspoon sesame seeds
salt and black pepper
vegetable oil, for deep-frying

Whiz the fava beans and chickpeas in a food processor until very fine. Remove and set aside in a large bowl.

Whiz the onion, pepper, fresh cilantro and garlic in the food processor until fine, then add to the beans and chickpeas along with the cumin, ground coriander, baking soda, sesame seeds, salt and pepper and mix well with your hands. Add enough water to make a smooth dough and set aside, 15 minutes.

Heat the oil in a deep-fat fryer or deep, heavy-bottomed saucepan. Mold the mixture into balls with your hands or using an ice-cream scoop. Gently lower into the hot oil and fry until browned.

Serve with pita bread, *tarator* (tahini sauce) (see recipe on page 140), pickles and salad.

If you were eating this in Lebanon, you probably wouldn't use the chili peppers – it's more traditional to season with things like cilantro. But when I started cooking in the UK, I learned to add chili pepper to dishes like this to add color and flavor, and now I prefer potatoes this way.

Serves 4

vegetable oil, for deep-frying
2 lbs potatoes, peeled and chopped into $^1/_2$-inch cubes
$^1/_4$ cup olive oil
$^1/_2$ onion, finely chopped
1 teaspoon minced garlic
1 red bell pepper, seeded and finely chopped
2 green chili peppers, finely chopped
1 tablespoon finely chopped fresh cilantro
salt and black pepper
$^1/_2$ teaspoon ground coriander

Heat the oil in a deep-fat fryer or deep, heavy-bottomed saucepan. Deep-fry the potatoes until crisp. Drain and set aside.

Meanwhile, heat the olive oil in a pan and fry the onion, garlic, bell pepper, chili peppers and fresh cilantro until softened. Add the potatoes along with salt, pepper and ground coriander to taste. Stir to combine and serve.

## sawda dajaj
### fried chicken livers

This is a really popular dish in Lebanon. We don't often go out to restaurants in Lebanon, but if we do eat out, we go to snack bars and eat wraps. These fried chicken livers are a common filling; liver is very popular in Lebanon. In fact, it is traditional to eat raw lamb's liver – it is eaten immediately after slaughter, while it is still warm. You wrap a chunk of the liver in bread, dip it in salt and pepper and put it straight in your mouth. I did eat it this way as a child, but these days I prefer my liver cooked, as in the recipe below!

Serves 2

1/4 cup vegetable oil, for frying
1/4 lb chicken livers
salt and black pepper
juice of 1/2 lemon
1 teaspoon pomegranate molasses
1 tablespoon garlic sauce (see recipe on page 140)

Heat the oil over high heat in a frying pan so it is about 1 inch deep. When hot, add the chicken livers and stir continuously until cooked, about 15–20 minutes.

Drain the oil from the pan, then add salt, pepper, the lemon juice, pomegranate molasses and garlic sauce and stir for a couple of minutes.

Serve hot with other appetizers and toasted bread.

عرايس الكفتة

Because of the climate in Lebanon, we do a lot of our cooking outside. This is a classic barbecue dish, and it's so simple to prepare. It's great if you need to feed a group of people fast. Cooking it over a charcoal grill makes all the difference, so don't make this on a gas barbecue.

Serves 4

1/2 lb finely ground lamb
1 tablespoon finely chopped onion
1 tablespoon finely chopped red bell pepper
1 tablespoon chopped Italian parsley
salt and black pepper
6 pita breads
2 tablespoons *tarator* (see recipe on page 140)
1 tablespoon pine nuts

Preheat the broiler to low.

Place the lamb, onion, pepper and parsley in a bowl. Add salt and pepper to taste and mix well.

Cut open each bread and spread a thin layer of the lamb mixture inside. Drizzle in a little *tarator* and add a few pine nuts to each. Close the breads and flatten them, then place under the broiler, turning, so as not to burn the bread before the meat is cooked. This should take about 5 minutes. Serve hot.

## makloubeh batinjan
### eggplant with meat and rice

*"Makloubeh"* means upside-down – this dish is prepared in a bowl and then turned out onto a plate to give a dome shape. You can use a big bowl as a mould or four smaller ones. One of my favorite eggplant recipes!

Serves 4

4 large eggplants
vegetable oil, for deep-frying
2 tablespoons olive oil
$1/2$ onion, finely chopped
$1/2$ lb lamb shoulder, chopped into 1-inch chunks
$1^1/2$ cups basmati or long-grain rice, soaked for 20 minutes
salt and black pepper
2 cups shelled peanuts, almonds or cashews

Peel the eggplants lengthwise with a potato peeler, leaving long stripes of skin. Cut one into cubes and the other three into thin slices.

Heat the vegetable oil in a deep-fat fryer or deep, heavy-bottomed saucepan. Deep-fry the sliced eggplants until browned, then remove and set aside, reserving the oil in the pan. Repeat with the cubed eggplant.

Heat the olive oil in a pan and fry the onion until softened. Stir in the meat and cook until browned, then add the cubed eggplant and 3 cups of water. Cook over low heat until the water colors, about 15 minutes.

Add the rice, salt and pepper and cook a further 20 minutes.

Meanwhile, deep-fry the nuts until golden. Watch that they don't durn. Drain and place in a serving bowl.

Line a large bowl with the eggplant slices. Pack the rice mixture in firmly, then place a large flat dish on top of the bowl. Turn out the eggplant "cake", being careful to keep its dome shape.

Serve the bowl of nuts alongside the eggplant cake. Serve with any type of salad.

**Kibbeh is a traditional Lebanese dish with several variations. Fine bulgur wheat is mixed with ground meat and spices, as below, or with potato, (kibbeh batata) and cooked. Kibbeh nayeh is the version made with raw meat.**

Serves 6

*for the stuffing*
2 tablespoons vegetable oil
1 onion, finely chopped
1/2 lb ground lamb
2 tablespoons pine nuts
salt and black pepper
1/2 teaspoon ground cinnamon

*for the dough*
1 1/4 lbs lean ground lamb
2 cups fine bulgur wheat, soaked in water for 15 minutes, then drained
salt
1 teaspoon kibbeh spices (available ready-mixed from Middle Eastern
   stores, or use a mixture of ground cumin, black pepper and salt)
1 medium onion
3 teaspoons ghee (clarified butter)

Preheat the oven to 350°F.

Prepare the stuffing first. Heat the oil in a saucepan and add the onion. Cook, stirring, until softened. Add the meat and cook until browned. Add the pine nuts, salt, pepper and cinnamon and cook a further 15 minutes, stirring all the time. Set aside to cool.

Next prepare the kibbeh dough. Whizz the meat in a food processor until smooth. Add the meat to the bulgur wheat along with the salt and spices. Whizz the onion in the food processor until fine, then add to the meat mixture. Mix well until it all sticks together.

Use some of the ghee to grease a large baking sheet with a rim and spread half of the kibbeh dough on the sheet in an even layer. Wet your hands and smooth the surface. Spread the stuffing over in another layer, then finish with another layer of the dough. Use a knife to cut the kibbeh into small squares, keeping them on the sheet. Dot with the remaining ghee.

Place the sheet in the oven and cook, 30 minutes. Serve with *laban* (yogurt) or *salatah khiar bi laban* (cucumber salad) (see recipes on pages 34 and 28).

kofta bil sainieh
kofta with eggplants and tomato sauce
كفتة بالصنية

**Kofta is the traditional way to serve meat in Lebanon. I like to keep this recipe classic. You can prepare this kofta in one big slice if you prefer, but it is nicer to do them in individual patties as below.**

Serves 4

1¹/₄ lbs ground lamb
¹/₂ onion, finely chopped
1 medium red bell pepper, seeded and finely chopped
2 tablespoons finely chopped Italian parsley
salt and black pepper
vegetable oil, for deep-frying
2 medium eggplants, peeled
2 tablespoons tomato paste, mixed in 1³/₄ cups water

Preheat the oven to 350°F.

Place the lamb in a bowl and add the onion, red pepper, parsley, salt and pepper. Mix all the ingredients together, then mold into 4-inch square patties about ¹/₂ inch deep. Place on baking sheets and bake in the oven, 10 minutes.

Heat the oil in a deep-fat fryer or deep, heavy-bottomed saucepan. Slice the eggplants into rounds and deep-fry until browned, then drain and set aside.

Remove the sheets from the oven and drain off any excess oil. Pour the tomato paste mixture over the patties and place an eggplant slice on each one. Return the sheets to the oven until the sauce has thickened, 30 minutes.

Serve hot with *roz abiad* (white rice) or *roz bil sha'rieh* (rice with vermicelli) (see recipes on pages 138 and 139).

كفتة مشوية مع اللبن

## kofta bil laban
### kofta with yogurt

**I was taught to make this dish by the head chef at Al Hamra in Mayfair and loved it, so I've always remembered the recipe and am happy to pass it on. This is a great way to present a dish – and in Lebanon we have a saying, "The eye eats before the mouth" – but as always, the taste is what's important, and this dish combines two classic Lebanese flavors.**

Serves 4
9–10oz ground lamb
2 tablespoons freshly chopped flat-leaf parsley, plus extra to serve
2 tablespoons onion, finely chopped
1 teaspoon seven spice mix (see page 43)
salt
2 pita breads
7oz plain yogurt (see recipe on page 34)
1 garlic clove, crushed
1 teaspoon tomato paste
1 teaspoon pine nuts
1 tablespoon butter or ghee (clarified butter)

Preheat the oven to 350°F. Make sure you have an oven-proof serving dish ready.

Put the lamb in a bowl and add the parsley, onion, spices and salt. Mix well, then form into finger-shaped pieces and grill over a hot grill for up to 10 minutes until cooked but still juicy. Set aside.

Cut some of the bread into triangular shapes (as shown) until you have enough to line the edge of your serving dish. Cut the rest into smaller pieces.

Mix the yogurt with the garlic in the serving dish. Stir in the small pieces of bread, then arrange the triangular pieces around the edge like a crown, as shown. Place in the oven for 10 minutes, watching it all the time, until the bread is golden-brown.

Cut the kofta fingers into small cubes. Heat the tomato paste in a small saucepan and add the kofta cubes. Cook together until the kofta is red. Add the pine nuts.

To serve, pour the kofta mixture over the yogurt and sprinkle parsley over the top.

أز بالفول واللحمة

roz bil foul wa lahme
rice with fava beans and lamb

**Fava beans are often used in Middle Eastern cooking – I always say we use them as much as Western cooking uses peas. The black pepper and salt are all the seasoning this lamb needs – its flavors are perfect on their own.**

Serves 4

**2 tablespoons olive oil**
**3/4 lb lamb shoulder, cut into large pieces**
**1/2 lb shelled fava beans**
**1 cup long-grain rice, soaked for 20 minutes and drained**
**salt and black pepper**

Heat the olive oil in a large saucepan and add the lamb. Cook over medium heat until the meat is tender, about 15 minutes.

Add the beans to the pan and cook for 5 minutes. Stir in the rice, along with 2 1/2 cups of water, salt and pepper.

Bring to a boil, then reduce the heat and cook until the rice has absorbed all the liquid, 15 minutes.

Turn into a serving platter and serve with *laban* (yogurt) (see recipe on page 34).

entrées **85**

**This is a meal in one, and is one of my favorite recipes. When I make this at home, my kids eat all the grape leaves – but the zucchinis are my favorite, so I don't mind! All you need is some *laban* (yogurt) (see recipe on page 34) to serve on the side.**

Serves 4

8 small zucchinis
3/4 cup Arborio rice
1/2 lb ground lamb
1 tablespoon ghee (clarified butter)
salt and black pepper
20 grape leaves (you can buy these in a jar from the supermarket)
6–7 lamb rib chops
juice of 3 lemons

Cut the stems off the zucchinis and hollow each one out. Rinse well.

Wash and drain the rice and place in a bowl. Add the ground lamb, ghee, salt and pepper and mix well.

Use the rice mixture to stuff each zucchini until it is three-quarters full, reserving some of the mixture for the grape leaves. Set aside.

Spread the grape leaves out on a plate, put a little stuffing in the center of each, tuck in the sides and roll up to make cigar shapes.

Place the lamb rib chops in one layer in the bottom of a large saucepan. Arrange the stuffed grape leaves in a ring in a tightly packed layer and place the stuffed zucchini in the middle. Use a plate that just fits inside the pan to press on top. Place a bowl of water on the plate to weigh it down. Pour in enough water to cover by about 2 inches and squeeze in the lemon juice. Bring to a boil, then reduce the heat and cook, about 1 1/2 hours. Drain.

Arrange the stuffed grape leaves and zucchini on a serving platter and serve hot.

# koosa wa batinjan mahshi bil banadorah
## stuffed zucchini and eggplants in tomato sauce

**Use the smaller-sized zucchini for this recipe. The western ones will be too big to stuff. Instead of throwing away the zucchini pulp try cooking it up with scrambled eggs – delicious!**

Serves 4

6 small zucchinis
6 small eggplants
1 cup Arborio rice, rinsed
$1/2$ lb ground lamb
2 tablespoons ghee (clarified butter)
salt and black pepper
4 tablespoons tomato paste, mixed in 4 cups water
1 teaspoon dried mint

Cut the stems off the zucchinis and hollow out. Rinse well. Do the same with the eggplants.

Place the rice in a bowl with the lamb, ghee, salt and pepper. Mix well.

Stuff each zucchini and eggplant with the rice mixture until three-quarters full. It's best to do this with your hands. Place in a large saucepan.

Pour in the tomato paste mixture, the dried mint and some salt. Use a heatproof plate that just fits inside the pan to push down on top of the stuffed vegetables. Place a bowl of water on top to weigh it down. Bring to a boil over medium heat, then reduce the heat and cook gently, 1 hour.

Remove the stuffed vegetables from the pan and transfer to a serving bowl. Top with any remaining tomato sauce. Serve hot.

*Kabsa* is a great one-pot dish and is perfect to prepare for a large group. Everything is cooked together – the rice, meat, nuts and raisins – which means it is both simple to make and full of flavor. *Kabsa* spice is available in Middle Eastern stores and some larger supermarkets, and is a delicious blend including cinnamon, black pepper and nutmeg.

Serves 8

3¹/₄ lbs leg of lamb
6 tablespoons vegetable oil
1 red bell pepper
¹/₂ large onion, finely chopped
2 garlic cloves, crushed
1 (14oz) can chopped tomatoes
1–2 chiles, chopped
1 lb ground lamb
5¹/₃ cups long grain rice, rinsed and soaked in lukewarm water
1¹/₄ quarts beef stock
3 tablespoons *Kabsa* spice
¹/₃ cup pistachio nuts, shelled
¹/₃ cup almonds
¹/₃ cup pine nuts

Preheat the oven to 350°F. Place the leg of lamb on a baking tray and coat with 3 tablespoons of the oil. Place in the oven for 90 minutes or until cooked, basting it with its own juices from time to time.

Meanwhile, place the red bell pepper on a separate baking tray and bake it in the oven for 15 minutes. Remove, let cool slightly, then peel and cut it into small pieces.

Heat the remaining oil in a large casserole with a lid. When hot, add the onion, garlic, tomatoes, bell pepper, chili pepper and lamb (in that order). Cook, stirring, for about 15 minutes until the meat is cooked.

Drain the rice and add it to the pan. Add the spices and salt and stir well. Pour over the stock. When it comes to a boil, cover and place in the oven with the lamb. Leave for about 30 minutes till the rice is cooked.

Meanwhile, boil and peel the pistachios and almonds and fry in a dry frying pan with the pine nuts for a few minutes until toasted.

To serve, carve the leg of lamb and arrange the meat on top of the cooked rice. Sprinkle over the nuts and serve with *laban* (yoghurt) (see recipe on page 34).

## frikkeh bil lahma
## roasted green wheat with lamb

**Frikkeh is roasted green wheat (see picture below) and it is a speciality of Lebanon. The people grow it, harvest it and roast it, which gives it a delicious smoky taste. This is a very typical village dish in Lebanon. You can try this dish with chicken instead of lamb if you prefer.**

Serves 4

$^1/_2$ lb roasted green wheat
$^3/_4$ lb lamb shoulder, cut into large pieces
2 tablespoons ghee (clarified butter)
1 medium onion, chopped
salt
2 cups nuts (such as pine nuts, cashews and blanched almonds),
  toasted until golden

Soak the wheat in a bowl of cold water 30 minutes. Skim off the dust that floats to the top and rinse in several changes of fresh water. Drain and set aside.

Meanwhile, bring a pan of water to a boil, add the lamb and cook until tender – this will take about 25 minutes. Drain, reserving the cooking water.

Heat the ghee in a separate pan, add the onion and cook until softened. Add the drained wheat and some salt and cook, stirring, 5 minutes.

Pour about $1^3/_4$ cups of the reserved cooking water into the pan, bring to a boil, then reduce the heat and cook gently until the wheat is tender but still has a bit of bite, 45 minutes.

Divide the wheat between serving plates. Arrange the cooked meat on top and scatter with the toasted nuts.

Serve with *laban* (yogurt) or *salatah lebnanieh* (Lebanese salad) (see recipes on pages 34 and 31).

## burghul bil lahma
## bulgur wheat with lamb

Like the *frikkeh bil lahma* on page 90, this is another typical village dish. It's very traditional and uses ingredients that are affordable for poorer Lebanese families.

Serves 6

2 tablespoons olive oil
2 tablespoons finely chopped onion
¼ lb lamb shoulder, cut into chunks
1 cup coarse bulgur wheat
salt and black pepper
¼ cup cooked chickpeas

Heat the olive oil in a saucepan, add the onion and stir until softened. Add the lamb and cook for 15 minutes until browned.

Stir in the bulgur wheat, salt, pepper and 2 cups water. Finally add the chickpeas and bring to a boil. Reduce the heat and simmer until the bulgur wheat is cooked, 30 minutes.

Serve with *laban* (yogurt) (see recipe on page 34) and salads.

## lamb

All entrées in Lebanon revolve around meat. Beef is the meat that is most commonly eaten at home, because it is cheaper than lamb. The fat-tailed sheep that are native to Lebanon are expensive because they are organically reared – it is actually cheaper to buy imported lamb from New Zealand. Personally I prefer lamb so I use it in all my entrées. I always grind my own lamb so that I know it will be of good quality.

The fatty tail of the fat-tailed sheep is a delicacy and is used in *kibbeh nayeh* – a very traditional recipe made with raw meat together with fresh basil and mint to add flavor. The fat is also threaded onto skewers with chunks of meat.

## khoudar bil lahma
### meat and vegetable stew

**You can use any vegetables you want in this stew, but carrot and zucchini are the classic choices. The meat becomes tender as it soaks up the spices and flavors. Adding the vegetables part way through stops them being overcooked, so they keep their texture.**

Serves 4

1 lb small potatoes, left whole
3 tablespoons butter
6 tablespoons vegetable oil
4 cups beef stock
3 tablespoons chopped onion
2 garlic cloves, crushed
1 leek, chopped
1 carrot, peeled and chopped
1 zucchini, cut into sticks
5oz button mushrooms, left whole
1 lb beef shank, cut into chunks
2 tablespoons tomato paste

Preheat the oven to 350°F. Place the small potatoes in a baking tray with the butter, half the oil, and 2 cups of the stock. Cook in the oven for about 30 minutes while you prepare the stew.

Heat the remaining oil in a large saucepan over medium heat. When hot, add the onion, garlic, leek, carrot, zucchini, and mushrooms (in that order).

Add the beef, stir and and cover the pan. Leave for 10 minutes until the beef is brown.

In a jug, stir the tomato paste into the remaining 2 cups stock. Add to the saucepan, stir and leave on medium heat for about 20 minutes.

Serve with the oven-baked potatoes.

## dajaj bil sabanikh
## chicken with spinach

دجاج بالسبانخ

**Spinach is grown all over Lebanon, but it is most commonly used in pastries, like the ones on page 67, and salad. This is a great family dish and very easy to make.**

Serves 4

2 tablespoons vegetable oil
2 tablespoons chopped onion
1 garlic clove, crushed
1 whole chicken, cut into 8 pieces
salt, to taste
5oz cooked chickpeas
$^1/_2$ cup pine nuts
1 generous cup chicken stock
9oz fresh spinach, finely chopped
juice of $1^1/_2$–2 lemons

Heat the oil in a large saucepan. When hot, add the onions first followed by the garlic. Stir for a couple of minutes, then add the chicken and stir well.

When the chicken is golden, season with salt and add the chickpeas, pine nuts, and chicken stock. Add the spinach and stir well, then cover and leave to simmer for 10 minutes.

Take off the heat, stir in the lemon juice and then serve with *roz bil sha'rieh* (white rice with vermicelli) (see recipe on page 139).

## dajaj meshwi bil hamod
### grilled chicken with lemon sauce

I learned to make this dish in the UK, but we make something similar in Lebanon. Adding oregano, mint and butter to the lemon sauce gives it a great flavor that works really well with the chicken. The more traditional way to prepare this would probably be in the oven, but for this version the easiest thing to do is to use a microwave, as below.

Serves 4

2 baby chickens, boned and halved
salt and black pepper
2 tablespoons butter
2 tablespoons flour
1/2 cup lemon juice
1 teaspoon oregano
1 teaspoon dried mint
2 tablespoons vegetable oil
1 large potato, sliced into chips

Preheat the oven's grill to high. Season the chickens with salt and pepper and then grill for up to 20 minutes until cooked. Set aside.

Melt the butter in a saucepan over medium heat. Add the flour and stir to form a paste. Add the lemon juice, oregano and dried mint. Season and continue to stir until the sauce thickens. Add a little water if needed.

Heat the vegetable oil in a frying pan over medium heat and fry the potatoes for 10 minutes until they are half cooked. Place the potatoes in a microwaveable dish, add the chicken and pour over the lemon sauce. Place the dish in the microwave on high for 5 minutes.

Serve with *roz bil sha'rieh* (rice with vermicelli) (see page 139).

Okra is very popular in Lebanon, but I have to admit that, growing up, I never really liked it! My mother used to cook it for us and, although my brothers and sisters loved it, I never wanted to try it. Now, though, I appreciate this traditional recipe, which mixes okra and lamb with garlic and cilantro – and if you like okra, you will love this.

Serves 6

1/4 cup olive oil
1/2 onion, chopped
7 garlic cloves, minced
1¼ lbs lamb shoulder, cut into large pieces
6 medium tomatoes, finely chopped
2 tablespoons tomato paste, mixed in 2 cups water
salt and black pepper
a large handful of cilantro, chopped
2 lbs okra (frozen is best)
juice of 1 lemon (optional)

Heat the olive oil in a saucepan, add the onion and garlic and stir until softened. Add the lamb and cook until browned, stirring occasionally. Stir in the tomatoes and cook over low heat, 5 minutes.

Pour in the tomato paste mixture, salt and pepper and bring to a boil, then reduce the heat. Add the cilantro and okra and cook a further 25 minutes.

Squeeze a little lemon juice on top if you wish, and serve with *roz abiad* (white rice) (see recipe on page 138).

# khoudar mahshi bil forn
## stuffed baked vegetables

**This dish uses Lebanese seven spice, or *Sabaa baharat* (see page 43). You could also try stuffing potatoes or eggplants, but my favorite stuffed vegetable is red bell pepper – I love the sweetness.**

Serves 6

1 tablespoon olive oil
2 tablespoons chopped onions
3/4 lb ground lamb
salt and black pepper
1 teaspoon Lebanese seven spice mix
1 tablespoon pine nuts
4 tomatoes
2 small red bell peppers
2 small green bell peppers
2 small yellow bell peppers
2 tablespoons tomato paste, mixed in 1 cup water

Preheat the oven to 350°F.

Heat the olive oil in a pan, add the onions and stir until softened. Add the lamb and stir until it changes color. Add the salt, pepper, Lebanese seven spice mix and pine nuts. Stir until the meat is cooked, about 20 minutes. Remove from the heat and set aside.

Cut the top off the tomatoes and scoop out the insides. Do the same with the peppers. Fill the vegetables with the lamb mixture and put their lids on top. Stand them in rows in a deep baking tray.

Pour the tomato paste mixture over the vegetables and season with salt. Cover the dish with foil and bake in the oven until cooked, 45 minutes.

Serve with *roz abiad* (white rice) (see recipe on page 138).

# daoud basha
## meatballs with pine nuts and tomato sauce

*"Basha"* comes from the Turkish word *"pasha,"* which was one of the higher ranks in the Ottoman Empire. It's equivalent to the British title of Lord. This dish is supposedly named after an Ottoman pasha who governed Mt. Lebanon in the 1800s. Perhaps it was his favorite dish – and these meatballs are certainly delicious.

Serves 4

2 lbs ground lamb
1 medium onion, finely chopped
1 cup pine nuts
salt and black pepper
vegetable oil, for deep-frying

*for the sauce*
2 tablespoons olive oil
2 medium onions, sliced
3 tablespoons tomato paste, mixed in 5 cups water

Place the meat in a bowl with the onion, pine nuts, salt and pepper and mix well. Mold the mixture into small balls.

Heat the vegetable oil in a deep-fat fryer or deep, heavy-bottomed saucepan, and deep-fry the meatballs until golden. Remove and set aside to drain on paper towels.

Now make the sauce. Heat the olive oil in a saucepan, add the sliced onions and stir occasionally until softened. Add the tomato paste mixture with salt and pepper. Bring to a boil, then reduce the heat and cook 30 minutes. Lower the meatballs into the mixture and cook for a few more minutes until heated through.

Served with *roz abiad* (white rice) (see recipe on page 138).

This is a really delicious dish, but I do prefer it with fresh lima beans, which are green and have a different texture and flavor. If you can't get hold of them, though, dried lima beans will also work well. You can use chicken breasts as an alternative to lamb if you prefer.

Serves 4

2²/3 cups dried lima beans
2 tablespoons vegetable oil
5 garlic cloves, chopped
3/4 lb lamb shoulder, cut into chunks
salt and black pepper
2 tablespoons tomato paste
2 tablespoons chopped cilantro
juice of 1/2 lemon (optional)

Bring the beans to a boil in a pan of water until half cooked, then drain.

Heat the oil in a large saucepan and cook the garlic until softened. Add the lamb, salt and pepper and fry gently until the meat is browned, about 15 minutes.

Pour in 4 cups of water, then add the tomato paste and cilantro and bring to a boil. Add the boiled beans, reduce the heat and cook gently, 30 minutes.

Squeeze a little lemon juice on top, if using, and serve with *roz abiad* (white rice) or *roz bil sha'rieh* (rice with vermicelli) (see recipes on pages 138 and 139).

**I learned this dish from my mother and she gave me the recipe. Some chefs prepare this with lamb as well as chicken but I prefer it this way, as my mother makes it. This dish does take some time, but it's worth it – the shallots and cinnamon give the chicken a great flavor.**

Serves 8

2$^1$/$_4$ lb *mograbieh* (giant, or Israeli, couscous)
1 chicken, cut into 8 pieces
salt and black pepper
6 tablespoons vegetable oil
2$^1$/$_4$ lb onions, chopped
10$^1$/$_2$oz can chickpeas
2 teaspoons caraway seeds
2 teaspoons cinnamon, plus extra to serve

Boil the *mograbieh* according to the packet instructions. Drain well and set aside.

Season the chicken pieces with salt and 1 teaspoon of black pepper. Heat 3 tablespoons of the oil in a frying pan over medium heat and add the chicken. Stir fry for a few minutes until browned, then transfer to a large saucepan.

Add the onion to the frying pan and fry it using the same oil you used for the chicken, then transfer this to the saucepan too.

Add 2 quarts of water, the chickpeas, and 1 teaspoon each of caraway seeds and cinnamon to the saucepan. Season with salt and stir. Cook over medium heat for 5 minutes to warm through.

Put the *mograbieh* in a large casserole dish. Add the remaining oil and spices, and stir on medium heat for 15 minutes.

Gradually add the chicken mixture until the liquid covers the *mograbieh*. Cook over low heat, stirring occasionally, until the *mograbieh* absorbs all the liquid.

Serve sprinkled with cinnamon.

**These stuffed cabbage leaves are extremely popular in Lebanon.**

Serves 4

**about 20 large cabbage leaves, separated**
**6 lamb chops**
**1 cup Arborio rice, rinsed**
**1¹/₄ lbs ground lamb**
**3 garlic cloves, chopped**
**salt and black pepper**
**3 tablespoons ghee (clarified butter)**
**juice of 2 lemons**

Boil the cabbage leaves in water for 2 minutes. Drain and set aside to cool. Boil the lamb chops in water for 5–10 minutes. Drain. Combine the rice in a bowl with the lamb, garlic, salt, pepper, and ghee. Spread the cooled cabbage leaves on a flat surface and divide the stuffing equally among them, fold in the sides of the leaf, then roll up in a cigar shape. Repeat with the other leaves.

Arrange the chops in one layer in the bottom of a deep saucepan then place the rolled cabbage leaves side by side in a circular fashion on top of the chops. Season with salt, then place a heavy lid on the cabbage rolls and add enough water to cover the plate by ³/₄ inch. Pour in the lemon juice and bring to a boil. Reduce the heat and cook, 1¹/₂ hours. Drain any excess liquid. Turn upside down onto a serving plate and serve hot.

A *Sheikh* is a holy person or leader, so the name of this dish really
celebrates the eggplant! Eggplants are one of my favorite foods, and this
has to be one of my favorite recipes in this book. Small eggplants are best
for this recipe.

Serves 4

12 small eggplants
vegetable oil, for deep-frying
1 tablespoon olive oil
1/2 onion, chopped
1/2 lb lamb
salt and black pepper
2 tablespoons tomato paste, mixed in 2 cups water

Preheat the oven to 350°F.

Peel the eggplants in stripes. Make a slit in each one lengthwise, about half
the depth of the eggplant.

Heat the vegetable oil in a deep-fat fryer or deep, heavy-bottomed saucepan.
Deep-fry the eggplants until golden, about 5 minutes (see picture on the
right). Set aside.

Heat the olive oil in a pan, add the onion and stir until tender. Add the
lamb, salt and pepper, and continue to cook until the meat is browned.

Place the eggplants in a deep baking tray and, using a teaspoon, stuff each
one with the meat stuffing.

Pour the tomato paste mixture on top of the eggplants, season with salt and
bake in the oven, about 15 minutes.

Serve with *roz abiad* (white rice) (see recipe on page 138).

# sanieh batata wa lahma bil ka'ak
## baked potato with meat and bread crumbs

**This is a very basic, straightforward dish that, to me, sums up the idea of Lebanese home cooking – simple ingredients, simple method, but wholesome and comforting. It looks like the Lebanese equivalent of Shepherd's Pie, but the pine nuts and breadcrumbs add crunch.**

Serves 6

2 tablespoons vegetable oil
1 medium onion, finely chopped
1/2 lb ground lamb
1 tablespoon pine nuts
salt and black pepper
4–5 large potatoes, boiled and mashed
3 tablespoons butter
1 cup dried bread crumbs

Preheat the oven to 350°F.

Heat the vegetable oil in a large skillet, add the onion and cook, stirring, until tender. Add the meat, pine nuts, salt and pepper and cook, stirring, until the meat is browned.

Place the warm mashed potato in a bowl, add 2 tablespoons of butter and some salt and mix well.

Grease a deep baking tray with the remaining tablespoon of butter. Spread half of the mashed potato in the tray. Spread the meat mixture over in one layer, then spread the rest of the mashed potato on top.

Sprinkle the bread crumbs on top and bake in the oven until golden, 20 minutes.

Cut into squares and serve hot or cold with salad or sautéed vegetables.

# kharouf mahshi
## roast leg of lamb

**If you want to feed a larger group of people, you can prepare this with a larger leg of lamb – you'll just need to adjust the cooking time. This is a great dish to prepare for a large group – traditionally, we would cook the whole lamb, served on a huge bed of rice, and everyone would gather around and eat together, tearing off chunks of meat with their hands.**

Serves 6

1 leg of lamb, roughly 2 lbs
salt and black pepper
1 tablespoon vegetable oil
1 medium carrot, chopped
1 medium red bell pepper, seeded and chopped
4 garlic cloves, peeled

Preheat the oven to 475°F.

Rub the leg of lamb with salt and pepper. Transfer to a deep baking tray and drizzle with the vegetable oil. Arrange the carrot, red bell pepper and whole garlic cloves around the lamb and pour in about 3 cups of water. Cover the tray with foil and roast in the oven, 1 hour.

Reduce the temperature to 350°F and cook for another hour. Check occasionally and top up with water if necessary.

Remove the lamb from the oven. Use a slotted spoon to remove the softened vegetables from the pan and place in a food processor. Add a little water and whizz to a smooth, runny gravy. Pour into a gravy boat.

Carve the lamb into slices and arrange on individual plates. Serve alongside the gravy and *roz abiad bil bazela* (white rice with peas) (see recipe on page 139).

## sanieh dajaj bil batata
## chicken with potatoes

**This is so basic and easy – it's all cooked in one dish and the potatoes soak up all the flavor of the roasted chicken. Serve this with plain white rice.**

Serves 4

1 whole chicken, cut into large pieces
salt and black pepper
2 tablespoons vegetable oil
1¼ lbs potatoes, cut into large chunks
juice of 1 lemon
4 garlic cloves, finely chopped

Preheat the oven to 350°F.

Place the chicken pieces in a deep baking tray, sprinkle with salt, pepper and oil and roast in the oven, turning regularly, 15 minutes.

Place the potatoes in with the chicken and pour in 1 cup of water. Cover the tray with foil and cook in the oven a further 40 minutes. Add the lemon juice and garlic and return to the oven a further 5 minutes. Leave to rest for 5 minutes before serving.

## shawarma dajaj
## chicken shawarma

شاورما دجاج

**Serve with mixed pickles (see recipes on pages 142 and 143), *toum* (garlic sauce) (see recipe on page 140) and pita bread.**

Serves 4

2 lbs chicken breasts
juice of 3 lemons
4 cardamom pods
salt and white pepper
generous ½ cup white malt or distilled vinegar

Cut the chicken pieces into long, thin slices. Put them in a deep dish with the lemon juice, cardamom pods, salt, pepper, vinegar and enough water to cover and leave in the refrigerator overnight to marinate.

Preheat the oven to 350°F.

Remove the chicken from the marinade and place on a baking tray. Cook in the oven, turning from time to time, 20 minutes. Serve.

*Shawarma* is very popular in Lebanon – it is the same kind of idea as the Turkish doner kebabs, but instead of fatty minced meat, slices of shoulder of lamb and spices are used – it is pure meat. This recipe is a good way of getting the same great taste at home. You will need to marinate the meat overnight so it takes on all the flavors of the spices. Mastic is an aromatic resin that is used to give flavor and is available from Mediterranean food stores.

Serves 4

1 shoulder of lamb
$^1$/$_2$ orange, sliced
1 lemon, sliced
1 onion
6 garlic cloves
1 bay leaf
pinch of cloves
salt
1 teaspoon mastic powder
1$^1$/$_2$ teaspoons shawarma spices (available from Mediterranean stores)
1$^1$/$_4$ cups malt vinegar
2 tablespoons lemon juice

Cut the meat into very thin, long slices.

Whizz the orange, lemon, onion, garlic, bay leaf, cloves, salt, mastic powder and spices in a blender until fine. Place this mixture in a deep dish. Add 3 cups of water, the vinegar and lemon juice. Coat the meat slices in the mixture and leave in the refrigerator to marinate overnight.

Preheat the oven to 350°F.

Remove the meat pieces from the marinade and place them in a deep baking tray, discarding the marinade. Cook in the oven, turning the pieces every now and then, 20 minutes.

Serve in pita bread with *tarator* (tahini sauce) (see recipe on page 140), pickles and tomatoes.

**Despite the name, you don't actually stuff the chicken in this recipe. This dish can be prepared by stuffing the chicken with the rice, but I prefer the simpler method of roasting the chicken and cooking the rice separately – it's much more straightforward and still tastes great.**

Serves 6

1 chicken (about 3$^1$/$_2$ lbs), cleaned
salt and black pepper
2 tablespoons vegetable oil
2 tablespoons olive oil
2 tablespoons finely chopped onion
$^1$/$_4$ lb ground lamb
$^1$/$_2$ cup pine nuts
1 cup long-grain rice
1 tablespoon flaked almonds, toasted

Preheat the oven to 475°F.

Season the chicken with salt and pepper. Place on a baking sheet and pour over the vegetable oil and scant $^1$/$_4$ cup of water. Cover the tray with foil and cook in the oven, 30 minutes.

Turn the oven down to 400°F and cook the chicken a further 30 minutes.

Meanwhile, heat the olive oil in a saucepan, add the onion and stir until softened. Add the lamb, pine nuts, salt and pepper, and stir until the meat is tender. Add the rice and stir. Pour in 1$^1$/$_4$ cups of water and bring to a boil. Reduce the heat and cook until the rice is tender, 15 minutes. Transfer the rice mixture to a serving platter.

When the chicken is cooked, cut into large pieces and arrange on top of the rice. Sprinkle with the almonds.

Serve with *laban* (yogurt) (see recipe on page 34) and salads.

# moulokhia bil dajaj
## jew's mallow with chicken

Jew's mallow is very popular in Lebanon. The plants look similar to mint, but have very long stems – they can grow to 5 feet high. In Lebanon people buy Jew's mallow leaves in the summer and dry it at home, spread out on their roof tops, in big batches of 20–30 pounds – it's extremely lightweight, so these batches are huge and last them for the year. I buy a big batch of fresh Jew's mallow when I visit Lebanon and dry it myself. You can get it in the US in Middle Eastern shops. This recipe is quite time consuming as you have to keep rinsing the mallow leaves until the water runs clear.

Serves 6

1/2 lb dried Jew's mallow leaves (*moulokhia* leaves)
2 lbs whole chicken
2 tablespoons vegetable oil
4 tablespoons ghee (clarified butter)
2 onions, finely chopped
3 garlic cloves, minced
1 tablespoon ground coriander
1 teaspoon dried red pepper flakes
a handful of chopped cilantro
salt
juice of 3 lemons

Soak the Jew's mallow leaves in water overnight. Drain and wash well until the water runs clear.

Place the chicken in a large pan of water and bring to a boil. Cook, skimming the scum from the surface every now and then, for 45 minutes to 1 hour. Drain and reserve the cooking water. Tear the chicken into pieces and set aside.

Heat the oil and ghee in a pan, add the onion and fry until softened. Add the garlic, ground coriander, red pepper flakes, fresh cilantro and salt. Cook gently for about 5 minutes, stirring. Add the Jew's mallow leaves and cook for 15 minutes over medium heat, stirring occasionally.

Add the chicken pieces, then pour in enough of the reserved chicken stock to cover by a couple of inches. Bring to a boil, then reduce the heat and cook about 45 minutes.

Squeeze the lemon juice on top of the *moulokhia* and remove from the heat.

Serve hot with *roz bil sha'rieh* (rice with vermicelli) (see recipe on page 139).

## khoudar bil dajaj
### spiced rice with chicken and vegetables

**The presentation of this dish makes an impressive feature on the dining table.**

Serves 4

2 tablespoons olive oil
1 tablespoon finely chopped onion
1 chicken, about 2 lbs, cut into large pieces
2 tomatoes, chopped
4 carrots, sliced lengthwise about 1-inch thick
$1/2$ teaspoon Lebanese seven spice mix (see page 43)
salt
4 zucchinis, sliced lengthwise about 1-inch thick
$2^1/3$ cups long-grain rice

Heat the olive oil in a large saucepan, add the onion and stir until softened. Add the chicken pieces and stir every now and then until the chicken starts to cook. Add the tomatoes and cook for 10 minutes, then pour in $2^1/2$ cups of water. Stir in the carrots, spice mix and salt and cook for a further 10 minutes. Add the zucchini and when cooked, use a slotted spoon to remove the carrots and the zucchini from the pan and set aside to cool. Add the rice to the pan, bring to a boil, then reduce the heat and simmer 30 minutes.

Use the carrot and zucchini strips to line a large bowl in alternating strips. Pack the rice in tightly, then turn out onto a serving plate. Serve with *laban* (yogurt) (see recipe on page 34) or salad.

In Lebanon, red mullet are quite small, about the length of a man's finger. They need to be small in order to fry them in this way. Small red snapper can also be used. Frying whole small fish like this is traditional in Lebanon – and coating them in flour first gives a satisfying crunch.

Serves 4

10–12 small red mullet, or red snapper, gutted and cleaned
salt and black pepper
5 tablespoons all-purpose flour
vegetable oil, for deep-frying
2 Lebanese breads (see recipe on page 136) or use store-bought pita breads
juice of 2 lemons

Sprinkle the fish with salt and pepper, then coat well with flour.

Heat the oil in a deep-fat fryer or deep, heavy-bottomed saucepan. Deep-fry the fish until golden, 10–15 minutes. Drain and place in a serving dish.

Cut the Lebanese bread into quarters. Fry in the same oil until golden. Drain and serve with the fish. Squeeze over the lemon juice and serve with *moutabal* (smoky eggplant dip) (see recipe on page 36).

This dish comes from Tripoli in North Lebanon, which is famous for *samak harra*. I use slightly different ingredients in my version. This goes beautifully with the *moutabal* (smoky eggplant dip) on page 36. You can use other fish if you prefer, such as salmon or sea bass. Use a cooking mat on top of the baking tray if possible – this will stop the fish from sticking.

Serves 6

1 (3$^1$/$_2$-lb) whole red snapper, gutted and cleaned
salt
ground cumin
handful of cilantro, finely chopped, plus extra for garnish
6 garlic cloves, minced
2 medium carrots, shredded
1 tablespoon finely chopped green chili pepper
1 tablespoon olive oil

Preheat the oven to 350°F.

Cut slits into the fish, then rub the fish inside and out with salt and cumin.

Combine the cilantro, garlic, carrot and green chili pepper in a bowl. Stuff this mixture into the cavity of the fish, then rub the fish with olive oil.

Place the fish on a baking sheet. Cover with foil and bake in the oven until the fish is golden brown on both sides, 1 hour.

Serve hot with *tarator* (tahini sauce) (see recipe on page 140) and cilantro to garnish.

# sayadieh samak
## fish with rice

The Arabic name of this recipe, *sayadieh samak*, comes from the Arabic for fisherman, *"sayad."* The fragrant cloves blend really well with the fish, and the finishing touch of the crispy browned onions is an added delight. This is good with the *tarator* (tahini sauce) on page 140 and salad.

Serves 4

2 lbs whole white fish, such as cod, sea bass, halibut, filleted (bones reserved)
2 tablespoons olive oil
$1^1/2$ onions, sliced
$^1/2$ cup pine nuts
salt and black pepper
6 cloves
$1^1/2$ cups long-grain rice
vegetable oil, for deep-frying

Place the fish bones in a pan with 2 cups of water and bring to a boil. Simmer to make a stock, 30 minutes.

Cut the fish fillets into large chunks. Heat the olive oil in a pan, add a third of the onions and fry until golden, then add the pine nuts to gently toast them. Add the fish and cook, 10 minutes. Add the strained stock, salt, pepper and cloves, then bring to a boil. Reduce the heat and simmer for about 10 minutes.

Add the rice and bring to a boil again. Reduce the heat and cook, 20 minutes.

Meanwhile, heat the oil in a deep-fat fryer or deep, heavy-bottomed saucepan. Deep-fry the remaining onions until browned and crisp. Drain.

Transfer the fish and rice onto a serving dish and scatter the browned onions on top. Serve.

This is a common sight in Beirut. For some people fishing is a hobby, while others make a living out of it. My brother used to fish like these people, spending all his day standing on the rocky seashore. Fishing is a hobby that needs a lot of patience because sometimes you spend hours and hours without catching even a small fish. People often stand there all day long and come home with nothing, but if they do catch something it might be a rabbit fish (a small fish with a nasty spike on the back of its head), black snapper or wrasse.

Another method people use is nets or cages that they put at the bottom of the sea. Different fish like different bait. You can use dough with a bit of sugar or shrimp – red mullet can be caught this way.

## sardin makli
### fried smelts

This is a very basic dish. It is eaten with toasted bread and *tarator* (tahini sauce) or *moutabal* (smoky eggplant dip) (see recipes on pages 140 and 36).

Serves 4

1¼ lbs whitebait (smelts)
salt and black pepper
¼ cup all-purpose flour
vegetable oil, for deep-frying
juice of 2 lemons

Rub the fish with salt and pepper, then coat well in flour.

Heat the oil in a deep-fat fryer or deep, heavy-bottomed saucepan. Deep-fry the whitebait until golden and crisp, 15 minutes. Drain, squeeze over the lemon juice and serve.

## kraidsieh makli
### fried jumbo shrimp with garlic and cilantro

Shrimp are very expensive in Lebanon, so this dish isn't eaten by everyone – only those who can afford to buy them.

Serves 4

1¼ lbs fresh jumbo shrimp, or frozen, thawed (about 12 shrimp)
1 cup all-purpose flour
salt and black pepper
½ cup vegetable oil
1 tablespoon lemon juice
5 garlic cloves, minced
2 tablespoons chopped cilantro

Peel the shrimp, remove the black vein that runs along the back, then wash well. Place the flour in a bowl with salt and pepper. Add the shrimp, coating them in the flour.

Heat the vegetable oil in a skillet and fry the shrimp, stirring occasionally, until cooked through, about 10 minutes. Drain the shrimp and toss with the lemon juice, garlic and cilantro. Season with salt and pepper and serve.

This dish is my own invention. I used to cook it for my brothers and whenever they came to me for dinner they would always request this dish! It is quite an indulgent dish, as saffron is expensive, but the flavors are fantastic.

Serves 4

3$^1$/$_2$ lbs fresh tiger shrimp or jumbo shrimp, or frozen, thawed
5 tablespoons olive oil
$^1$/$_2$ small onion, finely chopped
$^1$/$_2$ red bell pepper, seeded and finely chopped
$^1$/$_2$ green bell pepper, seeded and finely chopped
$^1$/$_2$ yellow bell pepper, seeded and finely chopped
1$^1$/$_2$ cups basmati rice
salt and black pepper
large pinch of saffron

Preheat the oven to 350°F.

Peel one-third of the shrimp, remove the black vein that runs along the back, then wash well. Cut into large chunks.

Heat $^1$/$_4$ cup of the olive oil in a deep pan and fry the onion over low heat for a few minutes. Add the chopped shrimp and fry, stirring occasionally, until half cooked. Add the peppers and cook until softened. Cover the pan when not stirring.

Add the rice, stir for a few minutes, then add 2$^1$/$_2$ cups of water, salt, pepper and half the saffron. Cover with a lid, bring to a boil and simmer over low heat, about 15 minutes.

Meanwhile, butterfly the remaining shrimp; leave the shells on, slice lengthwise but keep them joined at the tail end. Wash thoroughly. Place on a baking sheet, drizzle with 1 tablespoon of olive oil and sprinkle with salt, pepper and the remaining saffron. Bake in the oven, 15 minutes.

Serve the rice topped with the butterflied shrimp.

In the summer in Lebanon, we cook most of our meals outside on the barbecue. Over the weekend, families sometimes take their children to the nearest river. They bring meat and charcoals and set up a barbecue by the water. This grilled chicken has a strong garlic flavor that is delicious.

Serves 4

2 lbs chicken breast
1 tablespoon olive oil
1 tablespoon tomato paste
1 tablespoon minced garlic
1 tablespoon garlic sauce (see recipe on page 140), plus extra for dipping
salt and black pepper
juice of 2 lemons

Cut the chicken breasts into 1-inch pieces and place in a bowl. Add the olive oil, tomato paste, garlic, garlic sauce, salt, pepper and lemon juice. Mix well to coat the chicken and leave to marinate in the refrigerator for at least 1 hour or overnight.

Thread the chicken pieces onto skewers and cook for about 10 minutes on a barbecue or grill or under a preheated broiler, turning from time to time.

Serve with *toum* (garlic sauce) for dipping and a salad.

This is a simple dish – it just needs salt and pepper. For the best results, pepper the meat first, then cook, and salt it afterwards.

Serves 2

2 Cornish hens or squabs
salt and black pepper

Bone the Cornish hens (your butcher can do this for you). Rub with salt and pepper. Cook over charcoal for about 10–15 minutes, turning occasionally.

Cut the Cornish hens into quarters, then serve with *roz abiad* (white rice) and drizzle over *salsa harra* (hot sauce) (see recipes on page 138 and 141).

## kofta meshwi
### broiled ground lamb on skewers

كفتة مشوية

This is a very common barbecue dish – you'll see it served by butchers outside their meat stands (see opposite). The parsley, pepper and onion mixed in with the meat for this kofte gives it a great flavor. See the skewers on the right in the picture on page 128.

Serves 4

1¼ lbs ground lamb
1 medium onion, finely chopped
1 red bell pepper, seeded and finely chopped
a small handful of Italian parsley, finely chopped
salt and black pepper

Place the meat in a bowl with the onion, red pepper, parsley, salt and pepper. Mix well, then mold the mixture onto skewers and flatten a little with your fingers. Cook over charcoal for about 10 minutes, turning occasionally, and serve hot with salads.

## lahma meshwi
### grilled lamb on skewers

لحم مشوي

See the middle skewers in the picture on page 128. Serve this with a simple salad of very finely sliced onion, chopped parsley and sumac. Tomatoes and onions can also be grilled at the same time to add flavor to the meat.

Serves 4

1¼ lbs boned leg of lamb, cut into chunks
1 teaspoon tomato paste
1 tablespoon olive oil
salt and black pepper

Place the chunks of meat in a bowl and mix with the tomato paste, olive oil, salt and pepper. Refrigerate until needed.

Thread the meat onto skewers and cook over charcoal or under a preheated broiler, turning from time to time, 10–15 minutes. Serve immediately.

This guy looks like my grandfather! He had a shop like this in the meat market in Beirut a long time ago. I come from a family of butchers – including my uncles, grandfather and great-grandfather on my father's side. My father, despite going into a different business, is very knowledgeable about meat.

Butchers in the meat market sell skewers from barbecues set up outside their stalls. They have tables and chairs set out so you can sit and eat your skewer with pita bread. In Lebanon, everyone has a charcoal barbecue at home, usually on their balcony. I have a charcoal grill at home in London, a smaller version of the one I have in the restaurant – it was made for me by a friend. I use it in the garden in the summer. You can cook these recipes under a hot broiler at home but the taste just isn't the same and it certainly isn't authentic.

When I go to Lebanon I like to visit the meat market in a city called Nabatiyeh in the south. My grandfather's cousins have a shop there and now it is the younger generation who work there. Their barbecue meat is always fresh and tasty because it is bought from local farms. My family's place is nice and simple and I like to go there because it reminds me of when I was young at my grandfather's place in Beirut.

## kraidis meshwi
### broiled shrimp

قريدس مشوي

Shrimp are very expensive in Lebanon as they are not native to the country's waters. They are bred specially and are only available to those who can afford them. The lemon and garlic flavors of this recipe are delicious, but most Lebanese people would be more likely to eat fish (see below).

Serves 3

6 jumbo shrimp
salt and black pepper
juice of 1/2 lemon
1 teaspoon olive oil
3 garlic cloves, minced

Butterfly the shrimp; leave the shells on, slice lengthwise but keep them joined at the tail end. Wash thoroughly. Sprinkle the shrimp with salt and pepper, then place in a fish iron and cook over charcoal, turning from time to time so they cook evenly, 10 minutes. Place in a serving dish.

Mix together the lemon juice, olive oil and garlic to make a dressing. Pour over the shrimp and serve.

## samak meshwi
### broiled fish

سمك مشوي

Shrimp might be more expensive to get hold of, but anyone can go fishing in Lebanon's rivers! At home we would use black sea bream for this dish, but you can use any small white fish you like.

Serves 4

salt and black pepper
pinch of ground cumin
2 medium-size fish, such as sea bass and Dover sole, scaled and washed
2 tablespoons lemon juice
1 teaspoon olive oil
2 garlic cloves, finely chopped

Mix the salt, pepper and cumin together and rub over the fish and inside the cavity. Place the fish over charcoal and cook, turning from time to time, 20 minutes.

Mix together the lemon juice, olive oil and garlic and pour over the cooked fish. Serve with *salatah lebnanieh* (Lebanese salad) (see recipe on page 31).

As you will have learned by now, bread has to go with every meal in Lebanon! This Lebanese bread is made with very thin dough – thinner even than pita – and the amount of yeast makes it puff up as it cooks. This makes it easier to open. This dough can be used to make *khobez*, the traditional Lebanese bread shown in the picture on the right, and can also be used to make the breads on pages 69–71.

Makes about 15–20 breads

$4^1/_4$ cups all-purpose flour, plus extra for dusting
1 tablespoon sugar
1 teaspoon salt
1 tablespoon fresh yeast or cake yeast

Put the flour, sugar, salt, yeast and 1 cup of water in a large bowl. Mix together, then knead on a lightly floured board until you have a soft dough. Remove and divide into small balls about 2 inches wide. Place the balls on a wooden board. Cover with a moistened dishtowel and leave at room temperature to rise until they double in size, 15 minutes.

Dust the balls with flour on both sides and flatten with a rolling pin to form a circle about 1 inch in thickness. Place the circles back on the wooden board, cover with a moistened dishtowel and leave to proof for about 30 minutes or until about $^1/_2$ inch thick.

They are now ready to use for the dough recipes on pages 69–71. Alternatively, if using the dough to make Lebanese bread, place on a baking sheet and bake in an oven preheated to 400°F until golden and puffed up, about 5 minutes.

## ajeen sambousak
## pastry dough

Use this dough for *fatayer bil sabanikh* (spinach pastries), *sambousak jibneh* (cheese pastries) and *sambousak lahma* (meat pastries) (see recipes on pages 67, 66 and 65). It's good to make a big batch of the dough – anything you don't use can be saved and frozen. The pastries themselves keep well in the freezer so, again, freeze a big batch and have them ready for surprise visitors.

Makes enough for two batches of pastries

**9 cups all-purpose flour**
**1 teaspoon salt**
**1 teaspoon sugar**
**1 cup vegetable oil**

Place the flour into a dough mixer or food processor fitted with a dough hook. Make a well in the center. Add the salt, sugar and oil and process to a smooth mixture, about 15 minutes. Gradually pour in about 2 cups of lukewarm water, continuing to process in the mixer, until you have a dough the same consistency as bread dough.

Remove the dough and knead for a few seconds with your hands. Cut into two pieces and wrap in plastic wrap. Leave to rest at room temperature for about 1 hour before using.

## roz abiad
## white rice

This is a real staple and is served with almost every meal in Lebanon.

Serves 4

**1 1/2 cups long-grain white rice**
**salt**
**1 tablespoon vegetable oil**

Put the rice in a bowl, cover with warm water and leave to soak, about 30 minutes.

Fill a saucepan with water, add the salt and oil and bring to a boil. Drain the rice and add to the boiling water. Bring back to a boil, then reduce the heat and cook 10 minutes. Drain the rice of any excess water. Transfer to a serving dish and serve.

روز مع بازيلا

The peas add a splash of color and vary the texture and flavor. Serve with meat courses and barbecue dishes.

Serves 4

1 tablespoon olive oil
1/4 lb frozen peas
1 tablespoon finely chopped red bell pepper
1 tablespoon finely chopped green bell pepper
1 1/2 cups long-grain white rice, soaked in warm water 15 minutes
salt and black pepper

Heat the oil in a saucepan and add the peas and peppers. Cook about 5 minutes, stirring.

Add the rice to the pan along with salt and pepper and stir well. Pour in 1 3/4 cups of water and bring to a boil. Cover the pan, reduce the heat and cook for a further 15 minutes until the rice is tender and has absorbed all the water. Serve.

روز بالشعيرية

This is a popular rice variation in Lebanon. Serve with any main dishes with sauce, such as *moulokhia bil dajaj* (Jew's mallow with chicken), *bamia bil lahma* (okra with meat) and *fasoulieh bil lahma* (lima bean stew) (see recipes on pages 114, 97 and 101).

Serves 4

1 tablespoon olive oil
2oz vermicelli or angel hair pasta, crushed by hand
1 1/2 cups long-grain rice
salt

Heat the oil in a medium frying pan, add the vermicelli or angel hair pasta and fry until browned.

Pour in 1 3/4 cups of water and stir well. Add the rice and salt. Bring to a boil, then cover the pan, reduce the heat and cook until the rice is tender and has absorbed all the liquid, 15 minutes. Serve.

# toum
## garlic sauce

ثوم

**This is my wife's favorite. This recipe makes quite a large quantity, but it will keep in the fridge for a week. It's used as the base of the marinade for** *shish taouk* **(broiled chicken) (see recipe on page 129) and the sauce for** *sawda dajaj* **(fried chicken livers) (see recipe on page 76). If you have any left over, it is also good with chips!**

Serves 8 (makes enough to be used as a marinade in two recipes in this book)

2 garlic heads, cloves peeled
1 teaspoon salt
1 egg white
2 cups vegetable oil
juice of 2 lemons, or more to taste

Put the garlic cloves and salt in a blender or food processor and whiz to a smooth paste. Add the egg white and whizz again until smooth. With the motor running, very slowly pour in the vegetable oil in a constant, steady stream until all the oil is used up and the sauce is the consistency and color of mayonnaise. Add the lemon juice and keep whizzing until smooth. Taste and add more if necessary. Serve.

# taratour
## tahini sauce

طراطور

**Tahini is a classic Lebanese flavor – falafel just doesn't taste the same without it. It is served on the side with** *falafel* **(fava bean patties),** *sayadieh* **(fish with rice) and** *kofta meshwi* **(broiled ground lamb on skewers) (see recipes on pages 74, 120 and 130).**

Makes about 1/2 cup

3/4 cup tahini
salt
juice of 1 lemon

Place the tahini in a bowl. Add salt to taste, then gradually pour in about 1 1/2 cups of water, whisking, until it is the consistency of a sauce.

Whisk in the lemon juice and serve.

**Lebanese food isn't normally very spicy, but if you like a bit of heat then try some of this sauce. It is delicious served with grilled chicken or lamb dishes.**

Serves 8

1 tablespoon olive oil
1 tablespoon finely chopped onion
1 teaspoon minced garlic
1 tablespoon finely chopped red bell pepper
3 tablespoons finely chopped green chili pepper
1 (15oz) can (2 cups) plum tomatoes
salt and black pepper

Heat the olive oil in a pan. Add the onion, garlic, red bell pepper, and chili pepper and cook, stirring, 10 minutes.

Add the plum tomatoes, salt and pepper. Mix well, breaking up the tomatoes. Bring to a boil, then reduce the heat and simmer a further 20 minutes. Serve hot.

## kabis karnabeet
## pickled cauliflower

**When I make pickles I usually do five or six jars at a time as they last for a long time. You need to store different kinds of pickles in different jars. Beets are used to turn the vegetables pink.**

Makes 8 cups

1 large head of cauliflower, cut into small florets
1 cup malt vinegar
2 tablespoons coarse salt
1 small beet, sliced (optional)

Place the cauliflower florets in a 4-pint jar with an airtight lid.

Mix together the vinegar, salt and 4 cups of water. Pour into the jar and add the beet, if using. Close the jar tightly. The pickles will be ready to serve in 3–4 weeks.

## kabis malfouf
## pickled cabbage

**We eat pickles with almost every meal in Lebanon. Pickled cabbage and turnip (see opposite) are the most popular.**

Makes 8 cups

1 white cabbage
1 cup malt vinegar
2 tablespoons coarse salt
1 beet, sliced

Separate the cabbage into leaves and place them in a 4-pint jar with an airtight lid.

Mix together the vinegar, salt and 4 cups of water and pour into the jar. Add the beet and close the lid tightly. Leave for 3–4 weeks, after which it will be ready to use.

**The small French turnips are best to use. Don't use the big ones with tough skin – they don't work so well.**

Makes 8 cups

**10–15 small turnips**
**1 cup malt or distilled vinegar**
**2 tablespoons coarse salt**
**1 beet, sliced**

Cut the turnips into fat batons, the size of chunky fries. Place the turnip pieces in a 4-pint jar with an airtight lid.

Mix together the vinegar, salt and 4 cups of water and pour into the jar. Add the beet and close the lid tightly. Leave for 3–4 weeks before using.

**In Lebanon, we have wild cucumbers. They are pale green, stripey and curved. My mother always pickles them – but you can use small Western cucumbers too.**

Makes 8 cups

**10–15 small finger-size cucumbers**
**1 cup malt vinegar**
**2 tablespoons coarse salt**

Place the cucumbers in a 4-pint jar with an airtight lid.

Mix together the vinegar, salt and 4 cups of water and pour into the jar. Close the lid tightly and leave at room temperature for 3–4 weeks before using.

## ashtalieh
## cream pudding

This is my favorite dessert and is probably one of the most common made at home in Lebanon. We usually only eat desserts on special occasions – ordinary meals are followed by fruit and black tea. I use a brand called *Puck* for the cream cheese. It comes in 7oz cans and can sometimes be found in Middle Eastern stores. Otherwise any cream cheese will do. *Ashtalieh* will keep in the fridge for a couple of days.

Serves 6

4 cups milk
2 tablespoons sugar
5 tablespoons cornstarch
2 tablepoons all-purpose flour
3/4 lb cream cheese
2 teaspoons mastic powder
1 teaspoon orange blossom water
1 teaspoon rose water

*to finish*
1/2 cup pine nuts, soaked overnight in cold water
1/2 cup peeled almonds, soaked overnight in cold water
1/2 cup unsalted pistachios
*kater* (sugar syrup) (see recipe on page 149)

Heat the milk, sugar, cornstarch, flour and half the cream cheese in a saucepan over medium heat, stirring all the time with a whisk until the sugar dissolves. Bring to a boil, then reduce the heat and continue to stir until it thickens.

Add the mastic powder, orange blossom water and rose water and stir another 5 minutes.

Remove the pan from the heat. Pour the mixture into a shallow serving dish and set aside to cool. Spread the remaining cream cheese on top and store in the refrigerator until needed.

When ready to serve, divide into pieces, decorate with the nuts and pour over the sugar syrup.

This is similar to the *ashtalieh* (see recipe on page 146), but has a softer texture. The nuts are soaked overnight in water to soften them and give them a more subtle flavor. Finish with *kater* (sugar syrup) (see recipe below) if you like.

Serves 6

2 1/2 cups whole milk
2 tablespoons cornstarch
3 tablespoons sugar
1 tablespoon orange blossom water
1 tablespoon rose water
1 cup mixture of pine nuts, unblanched almonds and pistachio nuts, soaked overnight in water

Place the milk in a saucepan with the cornstarch and sugar. Bring to a boil, stirring all the time with a whisk. Reduce the heat and keep whisking for 10 minutes. Remove from the heat and stir in the orange blossom water and rose water.

Pour into serving dishes and leave to cool. Chill until ready to serve.

Drain the nuts and peel the almonds and pistachios, discarding the skins. Chop very finely, then sprinkle over the top of the puddings and serve.

Use in *ashtalieh* (cream pudding) (see recipe on page 146) or *mouhallabia* (milk pudding) (see recipe above).

1 cup sugar
1 teaspoon lemon juice
1 teaspoon rose water
1 teaspoon orange blossom water

Heat the sugar and 1/2 cup of water in a pan over medium heat until the sugar has dissolved.

Add the lemon juice and bring to a boil. Simmer for 2 minutes, then stir in the rose water and orange blossom water. Leave to cool.

## custard ma bescout
## custard with cookies

**My wife makes this for our kids and they love it. The biscuits soften in the custard. Best served very cold.**

Serves 8

1 quart whole milk
6 tablespoons custard powder
7 tablespoons sugar
3–4 tablespoons cocoa powder
15 graham crackers, crushed

Place the milk, custard powder and 6 tablespoons of sugar in a large saucepan over medium heat and bring to a boil, stirring all the time with a balloon whisk. Reduce the heat and cook for 15 minutes, whisking all the time until thickened.

Meanwhile, mix together the cocoa powder, remaining sugar and 1 tablespoon of warm water to make a paste. Spread the crushed crackers in a high-sided dish measuring 8in x 12in. Pour the custard over the cookies, then spread the cocoa paste over the top using a spatula. Refrigerate for 1 hour and serve.

## bae'lewa

*Bae'lewa* or "baklava" are sweets made from many layers of filo pastry, filled with nuts, such as almonds, pistachios, cashews, and brushed with sugar syrup. I haven't included a *bae'lewa* recipe because it is very complicated to make at home and you can easily buy good, inexpensive *bae'lewa*. The recipes in this chapter are the kind of desserts you might eat at home in Lebanon, whereas *bae'lewa* is saved for the most special occasions.

# riz bil halib
## rice pudding

رز بالحليب

**Not so different to the western-style rice pudding, but this one has rose water and orange blossom water for flavor and is finished with pistachios.**

Serves 6–8

**$1\frac{1}{2}$ cups Arborio rice**
**4 cups full-fat milk**
**$1\frac{2}{3}$ cups sugar**
**1 tablespoon rose water**
**1 tablespoon orange blossom water**
**5 tablespoons pistachios, soaked overnight in water and peeled, to serve**

Put the rice and $2\frac{1}{2}$ cups of water in a saucepan and bring to a boil. Reduce the heat and cook until the rice is half cooked, 10 minutes. Drain the rice.

Put the milk and sugar in a separate saucepan and bring to a boil, stirring all the time with a whisk. Reduce the heat and simmer, stirring constantly, 10 minutes.

Add the rice and cook, stirring all the time, a further 20 minutes. Remove from the heat and stir in the rose water and orange blossom water.

Pour into serving glasses and leave until cold. Scatter with the pistachios and serve.

**This is another popular Lebanese dessert. People don't always make it at home – they are more likely to buy it in sweet shops – but it's very simple to make. You can buy the** *osmalieh* **pastry dough in Turkish and Mediterranean shops – it is sometimes called** *kadayif*. **The cream has a secret ingredient: everyone who tries it will be amazed when you tell them it contains bread.**

Serves 8

$2^{1}/_{4}$ lbs *osmalieh* pastry dough
$^{3}/_{4}$ cup vegetable oil
1 tablespoon finely grated pistachio nuts
sugar syrup (see recipe on page 149), to serve

*For the sweet cream sauce*
$2^{1}/_{2}$ cups half and half
5 slices bread, toasted and crusts removed
1 teaspoon orange flower water
1 teaspoon rose water
2 tablespoons sugar syrup (see recipe on page 149)

First, make the sweet cream sauce. Pour the single cream into a saucepan. Crush the toast into fine pieces and add to the bowl. Whip the mixture until the toast blends into the cream.

Place the saucepan over medium heat and bring to a boil, stirring constantly. Lower the heat and add the orange flower water, rose water, and sugar syrup. When the mixture is firm, remove from the heat and allow to cool before use.

Preheat the oven to 350°F. Divide the *osmalieh* dough into two pieces. Put one piece at the bottom of a baking tray lined with parchment paper. Brush the top side with half of the oil and bake in the oven for 10–15 minutes until golden brown. Remove from oven and drain of any oil. Repeat the same procedure with the second piece of dough.

Put one piece of the cooked dough on a serving plate and spread the cream sauce on top, saving some for decoration. Top with the second piece of dough. Pour over the sugar syrup.

Pipe small blobs of cream on top and sprinkle with grated pistachio. Serve fresh.

## shai bil na'na
### mint tea

**Mint tea is good to drink at the end of a meal. In Lebanon we drink black tea for breakfast and mint tea after lunch or dinner.**

several mint sprigs
sugar (optional)

Bring a pan of water to a boil and add the mint. Simmer for about 10 minutes, then pour into a teapot. Pour into tea glasses to serve. Add sugar if you wish.

لبن عيران

## laban ayran
### yogurt drink

**This goes well with a meal, particularly dishes such as barbecued meat. You can add a little dried mint if you like but I prefer it without.**

Serves 4

1 lb yogurt (see recipe on page 34) or use store-bought plain yogurt
pinch of salt (optional)

Put the yogurt and salt in a bowl and whisk in 2 cups of cold water to a runny consistency. Set aside in the refrigerator for at least 1 hour to chill before serving.

You can buy packets of vacuum-packed Lebanese coffee in Middle Eastern shops. It is available with or without cardamom added, as you prefer. We use a *rakweh* to brew the coffee – it looks like a mini saucepan with a long handle. If you haven't got one, use a small saucepan instead. This coffee should be served without milk, like an espresso.

Serves 2

2 heaped teaspoons ground coffee
a few cardamom seeds, ground (if not already added to the coffee)
sugar, to taste (optional)

Put all the ingredients in a rakweh or small saucepan with scant $^1/_2$ cup of water. Place over medium heat and stir as you bring the mixture to a boil. Simmer, stirring all the time, for 5 minutes.

Pour into two cups and serve. The coffee grounds will sink to the bottom of the cups.

## kahwa arabieh

This coffee is made of the same mixture as the above recipe but there should be no sugar and more cardamom – the whole cardamom pod is used. The coffee is brewed in a large saucepan over a charcoal fire for three days, until the coffee grounds disappear. This makes it very intense and strong.

*Kahwa arabieh* is presented on special occasions such as wedding parties and funerals. When it is ready it is poured into decorative coffeepots, which are then offered with a tray of small cups for the guests. You take a cup of coffee and drink it and you are then offered a second. If you want one you hold your cup out, but if you don't want any more you should shake your cup.

People also go out and sell coffee in the streets from the coffeepots like you see in the picture. Charcoal is put in the top of the pot, which burns to keep the coffee hot.

desserts and drinks **155**

## Weight (solids)

| | |
|---|---|
| 7g | $^1/_4$oz |
| 10g | $^1/_2$oz |
| 20g | $^3/_4$oz |
| 25g | 1oz |
| 40g | $1^1/_2$oz |
| 50g | 2oz |
| 60g | $2^1/_2$oz |
| 75g | 3oz |
| 100g | $3^1/_2$oz |
| 110g | 4oz ($^1/_4$lb) |
| 125g | $4^1/_2$oz |
| 150g | $5^1/_2$oz |
| 175g | 6oz |
| 200g | 7oz |
| 225g | 8oz ($^1/_2$lb) |
| 250g | 9oz |
| 275g | 10oz |
| 300g | $10^1/_2$oz |
| 310g | 11oz |
| 325g | $11^1/_2$oz |
| 350g | 12oz ($^3/_4$lb) |
| 375g | 13oz |
| 400g | 14oz |
| 425g | 15oz |
| 450g | 1lb |
| 500g ($^1/_2$kg) | 18oz |
| 600g | $1^1/_4$lb |
| 700g | $1^1/_2$lb |
| 750g | 1lb 10oz |
| 900g | 2lb |
| 1kg | $2^1/_4$lb |
| 1.1kg | $2^1/_2$lb |
| 1.2kg | 2lb 12oz |
| 1.3kg | 3lb |
| 1.5kg | 3lb 5oz |
| 1.6kg | $3^1/_2$lb |
| 1.8kg | 4lb |
| 2kg | 4lb 8oz |
| 2.25kg | 5lb |
| 2.5kg | 5lb 8oz |
| 3kg | 6lb 8oz |

## Volume (liquids)

| | |
|---|---|
| 5ml | 1 teaspoon |
| 10ml | 1 dessertspoon |
| 15ml | 1 tablespoon or $^1/_2$fl oz |
| 30ml | 1fl oz |
| 40ml | $1^1/_2$fl oz |
| 50ml | 2fl oz |
| 60ml | $2^1/_2$fl oz |
| 75ml | 3fl oz |
| 100ml | $3^1/_2$fl oz |
| 125ml | 4fl oz |
| 150ml | 5fl oz ($^1/_4$ pint) |
| 160ml | $5^1/_2$fl oz |
| 175ml | 6fl oz |
| 200ml | 7fl oz |
| 225ml | 8fl oz |
| 250ml (0.25 litre) | 9fl oz |
| 300ml | 10fl oz ($^1/_2$ pint) |
| 325ml | 11fl oz |
| 350ml | 12fl oz |
| 370ml | 13fl oz |
| 400ml | 14fl oz |
| 425ml | 15fl oz ($^3/_4$ pint) |
| 450ml | 16fl oz |
| 500ml (0.5 litre) | 18fl oz |
| 550ml | 19fl oz |
| 600ml | 20fl oz (1 pint) |
| 700ml | $1^1/_4$ pints |
| 850ml | $1^1/_2$ pints |
| 1 litre | $1^3/_4$ pints |
| 1.2 litres | 2 pints |
| 1.5 litres | $2^1/_2$ pints |
| 1.8 litres | 3 pints |
| 2 litres | $3^1/_2$ pints |

## Length

| | |
|---|---|
| 5mm | $^1/_4$ in |
| 1cm | $^1/_2$ in |
| 2cm | $^3/_4$ in |
| 2.5cm | 1in |
| 3cm | $1^1/_4$ in |
| 4cm | $1^1/_2$ in |
| 5cm | 2in |
| 7.5cm | 3in |
| 10cm | 4in |
| 15cm | 6in |
| 18cm | 7in |
| 20cm | 8in |
| 24cm | 10in |
| 28cm | 11in |
| 30cm | 12in |

**A**

*adas bil hamed* 13
*ajeen al khobez* 136
*ajeen sambousak* 138
*arayes al kofta* 77
*ashtalieh* 146

**B**

baklava 150
*bae'lewa* 150
*bamia bil lahma* 97
*barassia* 54
barbecues 131
  barbecued hens 129
*batata harra* 75
*batinjan bi zeit* 43
*batinjan makdous* 42
*batinjan rahib* 46
beans
  beans in oil 50
  fava bean patties 74
  fava beans with garlic and cilantro 41
  lima bean stew 101
  lima beans with tahini sauce 21
  fava beans with garlic and chickpeas 58
  green beans with tomato 50
  rice with fava beans and lamb 85
bread 7, 73
  baked dough with cheese 70
  bread baked with thyme 7, 69
  bread dough 136
  broiled pita bread stuffed with meat 77
  small meat pizzas 71
  toasted bread salad 38
*burghul bil lahma* 92

**C**

cabbage
  pickles cabbage 142
  stuffed cabbage leaves 103
  white cabbage salad 30
carrots 44
cauliflower 142
chard
  lentil soup with Swiss chard and
    lemon 13
  stuffed Swiss chard leaves 55
cheese pastries 66
cheese with baked dough 70

chicken 7
  barbecued hens 129
  broiled chicken 7, 129
  chicken shawarma 110
  chicken soup with vermicelli/angel hair
    pasta 14
  chicken with potatoes 110
  chicken with spinach 94
  grilled chicken with lemon sauce 96
  fried chicken livers 76
  Jew's mallow with chicken 114
  spiced rice with chicken and vegetables
    116
  stuffed chicken with rice 113
chickpeas
  chickpea dip 35
  chickpea dip with lamb and pine
    nuts 61
  fava beans with garlic and chickpeas 58
chicory in olive oil 51
chile
  ground nuts with chile 37
  hot sauce 141
  Lebanese chile fish 119
coffee 155
cilantro 41, 122
cream pudding 146
cucumber
  cucumber and yogurt dip 28
  pickled cucumber 143
*custar ma bescout* 150
custard with cookies 150

**D**

*dajaj bil sabanikh* 94
*dajaj mahshi bil roz* 113
*dajaj meshwi bil hamod* 96
*daoud basha* 100

**E**

eggplant
  eggplant and tomato moussaka 52
  eggplant salad 46
  eggplant with meat and rice 80
  kofta with eggplants and tomato
    sauce 83
  Lebanese stuffed eggplant 105
  pickled eggplant 42
  smoky eggplant dip 7, 36

stuffed eggplants in oil 43
stuffed zucchini and eggplants in
 tomato sauce 88

**F**

*falafel* 74
*farrouge meshwi* 129
*fasoulieh bi zeit* 50
*fasoulieh bil lahma* 101
*fasoulieh bil tahini* 21
*fatayer bil sabanikh* 67
*fattoush* 38
fish 7, 121
 broiled fish 132
 crispy fried fish 117
 fish with rice 120
 fried smelts (whitebait) 122
 Lebanese chile fish 119
*foul medames* 58
*foul moukala* 41
*fouter moukala* 41
*frikkeh bil lahma* 90

**G**

garlic 7
 fava beans with garlic and cilantro 41
 fava beans with garlic and chickpeas 58
 fried jumbo prawns with garlic and
  cilantro 122
 fried mushrooms with garlic and
  cilantro 41
 garlic sauce 140
grains 7
grape leaves
 stuffed zucchini and grape leaves 87
 stuffed grape leaves in oil 49

**H**

halloumi with za'atar 59
herbal tea 15
*hindbieh bi zeit* 51
*hummus awarma* 61
*hummus bil tahina* 35

**J**

Jew's mallow 44
 Jew's mallow with chicken 114
*jibneh bil za'atar* 59

**K**

*kabis karnabeet* 142
*kabis khiar* 143
*kabis lift* 143
*kabis malfouf* 142
*kabsa* 89
*kahwa arabieh* 155
*kahwa lebnanieh* 155
*kater* 149
*kharouf mahshi* 108
*khoudar bil dajaj* 116
*khoudar bil lahma* 93
*khoudar mahshi bil forn* 98
*kibbeh bil sainieh* 82
*kofta bil sainieh* 83
*kofta bil laban* 84
*kofta meshwi* 130
*koosa wa batinjan mahshi bil banadorah* 88
*koosa wa warak einab mahshi* 87
*kraidis meshwi* 132
*kraidsieh* 125
*kraidsieh makli* 122

**L**

*laban* 34
*laban ayran* 154
*lahma bi ajeen* 71
*lahma meshwi* 130
lamb 7, 92
 eggplant with meat and rice 80
 baked kibbeh 82
 baked potato with meat and
  bread crumbs 106
 bulgur wheat with lamb 92
 chickpea dip with lamb and pine
  nuts 61
 broiled lamb on skewers 130
 broiled ground lamb on skewers 130
 broiled pita bread stuffed with meat 77
 kofta with eggplants and tomato
  sauce 83
 kofta with yogurt 84
 meatballs with pine nuts and tomato
  sauce 100
 meat pastries 65
 meat shawarma 111
 rice with fava beans and lamb 85
 roast leg of lamb 108
 roasted green wheat with lamb 90

 small meat pizzas 71
Lebanese coffee 155
Lebanese couscous 102
Lebanese salad 31
leeks in oil 54
lemons 13, 44
lentil soup 10
lentil soup with Swiss chard and lemon 13
lentils and rice with crispy onions 62
*loubia bi zeit* 50

**M**

*makloubeh batinjan* 80
*malfouf mahshi* 103
*manakeish bil jibneh* 70
*manakeish bil zahtar* 7, 69
markets 44–45
meat and spiced rice stew 89
meat and vegetable stew 93
milk 34, 146
 milk pudding 149
mint tea 154
*mograbieh* 102
*mouhallabia* 149
*moujadara* 62
*moulokhia bil dajaj* 114
*moussaka bi zeit* 52
*moutabal* 7, 36
*muhamara* 37
mushrooms fried with garlic and
 cilantro 41

**N**

nuts 73
 chickpea dip with lamb and pine
  nuts 61
 ground nuts with chile 37
 meatballs with pine nuts and tomato
  sauce 100

**O**

okra with meat 97
olive 7
 beans in oil 50
 chicory in olive oil 51
 leeks in oil 54
 okra in oil 54
 olive salad 25
 olive trees 25

stuffed eggplants in oil 43
  stuffed grape leaves in oil 49
onion and tomato salad 28
onions with lentils and rice 62
*osmalieh* 152

**P**
parsley 44
  parsley salad 7, 48
pastry dough 138
peas with white rice 139
pickled eggplants 42
pickled cabbage 142
pickled cauliflower 142
pickled cucumber 143
pickled turnip 143
potatoes
  baked potato with meat and
    bread crumbs 106
  chicken with potatoes 110
  potato salad 22
  spicy potatoes 75

**R**
radish and arugula salad 21
rice
  eggplant with meat and rice 80
  fish with rice 120
  lentils and rice with crispy onions 62
  rice with fava beans and lamb 85
  rice pudding 151
  rice with vermicelli 139
  spiced rice and meat stew 89
  spiced rice with chicken and vegetables
    116
  stuffed chicken with rice 113
  tiger shrimp with rice and vegetables 125
  white rice 138
  white rice with peas 139
  *riz bil halib* 151
  arugula salad with radishes 21
  *roz abiad* 138
  *roz abiad bil bazela* 139
  *roz bil foul wa lahme* 85
  *roz bil sha'rieh* 139

**S**
*salatah al khodar al meshweya* 26
*salatah harra* 31

*salatah khiar bi laban* 28
*salatah lebnanieh* 31
*salatet al banadorah wa al basal* 28
*salatet rocca* 21
*salatet zaytoon* 25
*salatit batata* 22
*salatit malfouf abiad* 30
*salatit zahtar akhdar* 30
*salsa hara* 141
*samak harra* 119
*samak makli* 117
*samak meshwi* 132
*sambousak jibneh* 66
*sambousak lahma* 65
*sanieh batata wa lahma bil ka'ak* 106
*sanieh dajaj bil batata* 110
*sardin makli* 122
*sawda dajaj* 76
*sayadieh samak* 120
*shai bil na'na* 154
*shawarma bil lahma* 111
*shawarma dajaj* 110
*sheikh mahshi* 105
*shish taouk* 7, 129
*shorbet adas* 10
*shorbet al khoudar bil sha'rieh* 16
*shorbet al khoudar* 13
*shorbet dajaj bil sha'rieh* 14
shrimp
  fried jumbo shrimp with garlic and
    cilantro 122
  broiled shrimp 132
  tiger shrimp with rice and vegetables 125
*silic bi zeit* 55
spices 45
  spiced rice and meat stew 89
  spiced rice with chicken and vegetables
    116
  spicy hot salad 31
  spicy potatoes 75
spinach pastries 67
spinach with chicken 94
street snacks 73
sugar syrup 149
sumac 38

**T**
*tabbouleh* 7, 48
tahini sauce 21, 140

*taratour* 140
tea 15, 154
thyme 7, 69
  fresh thyme salad 30
tomatoes
  eggplant and tomato moussaka 52
  kofta with eggplants and tomato
    sauce 83
  meatballs with pine nuts and tomato
    sauce 100
  stuffed zucchini and eggplants in
    tomato sauce 88
tomato and onion salad 28
*toum* 140
turnip 143

**V**
vegetables 7, 44
  broiled vegetable salad 26
  spiced rice with chicken and vegetables
    116
  stuffed baked vegetables 98
  tiger shrimp with rice and vegetables 125
  vegetable soup 13
  vegetable soup with vermicelli 16
vermicelli and chicken soup 14
vermicelli dessert 152
vermicelli with rice 139

**W**
*warak einab bi zeit* 49
wheat
  bulgur wheat with lamb 92
  roasted green wheat with lamb 90

**Y**
yogurt 34
  yogurt drink 154
  yogurt with cucumber dip 28
  yogurt with kofta 84

**Z**
zucchini 44
  stuffed zucchini and eggplant in
    tomato sauce 88
  stuffed zucchini and grape leaves 87

**Hussien Dekmak** was born in Beirut and has been cooking since he was a teenager. He trained at Al Hamra in London's West End, and opened Le Mignon in 1997 – "an outpost of classic Lebanese cooking in Camden" (*Time Out London*). He is now the head chef at the Mia Lounge restaurants in London.

## Picture credits

All photography by Martin Brigdale except the following:

Page 6 (top left, top right, bottom right) Hussien Dekmak
Page 15 Bethune Carmichael / Lonely Planet
Page 25 Edward Parker / Alamy
Page 44 Roger Wood / Corbis
Page 45 (top) Robert Harding Picture Library Ltd / Alamy
Page 45 (bottom) Ali Kabas / Alamy
Page 72 (top) John Wreford / Alamy
Page 72 (bottom) Robert Harding Picture Library Ltd / Alamy
Page 73 World Religions Photo Library,
  www.middleeastpictures.com / Laurence Mitchell
Page 92 Char Abumansoor / Alamy
Page 121 John Wreford / Arabian Eye
Page 131 Helene Rogers / Alamy
Page 150 World Religions Photo Library,
  www.middleeastpictures.com / Christine Osborne
Page 155 Roger Wood / Corbis

## Acknowledgments

Thanks go to:

• Kyle Cathie for giving me the chance to introduce this book
• Jenny Wheatley, my editor, for all her help and support
• Martin Brigdale for taking the beautiful photographs
• Helen Trent for all the art that made my cooking look great
• The team at Kyle Cathie Ltd for all their hard work
• My brother Samir for his support and confidence
• Mr. Samir Balaghi for his advice
• The many chefs at Al Hamra restaurant I have worked with for teaching me a lot about food
• Zaid Hamandi for supplying all the ingredients for my recipes
• All my friends for supporting me
• All the clients who have eaten my food
• My mother and father for their continuous love and support
• My youngest brother Oussama for his help and all our good work at Le Mignon
• My sister Naife for her help
• My wife Benan for all her love and support